Suddenly, the Cider Didn't Taste So Good

John Ford Sr.

ISLANDPORT PRESS

Islandport Press
P.O. Box 10
Yarmouth, Maine 04096
www.islandportpress.com
books@islandportpress.com

Copyright © 2012 by John Ford Sr.
First Islandport Press edition published April 2012.

All Rights Reserved.

ISBN: 978-1-934031-94-0
Library of Congress Card Number: 2011935469

Book jacket design by Karen F. Hoots / Hoots Design
Book designed by Michelle A. Lunt / Islandport Press
Publisher Dean L. Lunt
Cover image of courtesy of Dean L. Lunt

Suddenly, the Cider Didn't Taste So Good

Also from Islandport Press

Tales from Misery Ridge by Paul J. Fournier

Where Cool Waters Flow by Randy Spencer

My Life in the Maine Woods by Annette Jackson

Nine Mile Bridge by Helen Hamlin

Old Maine Woman by Glenna Johnson Smith

Abbott's Reach by Ardeana Hamlin

Shoutin' into the Fog by Thomas Hanna

Contentment Cove and *Young* by Miriam Colwell

Stealing History and *Breaking Ground* by William D. Andrews

Windswept, Mary Peters, and *Silas Crockett* by Mary Ellen Chase

Mercy, The Last New England Vampire by Sarah L. Thomson

In Maine by John N. Cole

The Cows Are Out! by Trudy Chambers Price

Hauling by Hand by Dean Lawrence Lunt

A Moose and a Lobster Walk into a Bar by John McDonald

The Cat at Night by Dahlov Ipcar

My Wonderful Christmas Tree by Dahlov Ipcar

Farmyard Alphabet by Dahlov Ipcar

These and other Maine books are available at:
www.islandportpress.com

I dedicate this book to all of the wardens, past and present, and to their families for the many sacrifices made while serving the sportsmen of Maine. Fifteen have made the ultimate sacrifice doing a job they loved. Lest we never forget them.

And, I offer a special dedication to retired Maine Game Warden Vernon Walker and my mother, Ethelind Walker. It was their inspiration and encouragement that allowed my dream of one day becoming a game warden to become a reality. I am forever indebted to their memory.

Acknowledgments

I would like to personally thank my wife, Judy, and my son, John Jr., for putting up with my crazy antics, those sometimes out-of-control rants, and the many hours of discourse in their own lives as I pursued my career. Without their complete support, understanding, and patience, my career would never have been as enjoyable as it was. They too have sacrificed.

The wardens I worked with and their wives also deserve mention, for they have their own stories to share, many of them probably far more interesting than my own. The wardens' wives seldom get the credit they deserve for their faithful support, sacrifices, and dedication to the agency and to the sportsmen of Maine.

A special thanks to *Morning Sentinel* editor Beth Staples and to *Village Soup* editor Jay Davis for their encouragement in moving this project forward to the point where it has finally been published.

And finally, to the sportsmen of Maine, who, even though some find themselves in conflict with the rules, continue establishing the good old tradition of The Maine Way of Life. Without them, there would have been no memories. Thank you, all!

Table of Contents

Foreword

I first met John Ford Sr. about two days after he started working for the Maine Warden Service in 1970. He was a small-town boy from Sanford with warden ties who, at an early age, was able to occasionally accompany Verne Walker, Charlie Libby, and Don Gray as they patrolled their districts. In a small way, he was able to experience firsthand the many duties and activities of a Maine Game Warden.

I'd grown up with the Warden Service myself and had accepted it as a way of life. My father, Maynard Marsh, had been chief warden in the 1970s, prior to becoming commissioner. In later years, I also found myself occupying the chief warden's position.

One of the veteran officers who knew John was well aware of his background and voiced skepticism as to his commitment. He said John would probably be back in Sanford before Christmas, which was coming right up.

I knew John's stepfather, Verne Walker, who I regarded as a good district warden. I knew if John was following in his footsteps, he had a leg up on the others.

Back in those days it helped to get hired if you knew a game warden. Then the department gave you a .38 Smith & Wesson handgun, an old sedan, and a trunk full of new equipment and sent you off to work with a veteran warden in someplace you'd likely never heard of. If you were fortunate enough to last a year or two, you were sent to a basic school where you'd learn from men who'd been active game wardens for fifteen or twenty years.

Your office was your house, your wife was the unpaid secretary. Complaints were phoned straight to your home, not through a central dispatch system like today. If you were there, you answered the call. If you weren't, your wife would call the store or the gas station where you might be patrolling and leave a message. There were no radios, no handheld portables; it was pretty primitive, but it all was about to change when John came aboard.

To the best of my knowledge, John had never set a trap and he wasn't a big deer hunter, but he learned to take care of the traditional things while adapting to the new responsibilities, such as watercraft and snowmobiles and environmental issues. For many years, being a game warden was pretty simple. For one thing, the job description mentioned working a "nonstandard work week," which was considered to be the time it took to get the job done. Often, that meant patrolling during the day and chasing night-hunters almost until the morning of the next day, and then you started the process all over. We did it not for the meager paycheck, but because we liked it.

John was assigned to Waldo County's Burnham area, about fifteen miles northeast of Waterville, a busy place to be a warden. He was twenty-two years old and replacing a man whose house was shot up by some yahoos while his wife and young daughter were there. Nobody got hurt, thankfully, but we decided it would be best to put a single man in that district. John was eager to go anywhere and he was single, so he certainly fit the bill. It was his chance to prove himself or return to Sanford from whence he came. Obviously, he was able to prove himself.

The Burnham area had the largest concentration of deer per acre in the state, along with many families of low socioeconomic status. They were folks who lived pretty close to the land. They killed game in order to help them get by, and they were not always legal in their efforts. It was certainly a different assignment than most other places. For example, you'd go to the store to fill up your gas tank and the proprietor would quickly wait on you because he had to, but he wasn't all that friendly. It seemed like he was in a rush to get you out of there before the regular customers came along.

Most wardens throughout the state came from a farm or forestry background, or they were hunters, trappers, or fishermen. But John was looked upon as a flatlander from southern Maine—I believe his biggest interest in high school was girls—and he was as green as they come as far as warden work. I'll give you an example. Early in his career he was covering a car-deer accident when a state trooper contacted him to see if he needed photos. The State Police always sent someone to take pictures if there was a fatality involved. The deer was killed in this collision so John said, "Sure, send the photographer." We still laugh about that incident to this very day.

But he was pretty sharp, too. Back then Mount Desert Island was overrun with deer, and the state was considering a substantial reduction of the herd, which was controversial to say the least. To help justify the project, the state got the University of Maine involved and conducted an experiment on how we could establish what time a deer had died. Some

of the research was done in Waldo County, and John was
very interested in that effort. He was willing to tackle a new
method of enforcement. Wardens were used to writing summonses for incidents they saw happening right in front of
them. But now, if they could tell how long a deer had been
dead, they could officially charge a hunter with a crime
going back in time. John bit onto this scientific discovery in
a continuation of his persistent pursuit of night-hunters.

I will also vouch for his tenacity as an investigator. In
the late 1960s, the state required all hunters to wear blaze
orange in an attempt to reduce the many hunting fatalities
that had reached forty or more in some seasons. But the
practice was new and unpopular among hunters who seriously believed that no deer would ever get close enough for
them to shoot if they wore the mandatory bright colors.

There was a hunter in John's territory who was wearing
an orange hat when he was shot in the arm by a man who
mistook him for a deer. The wounded man was an opponent
of the blaze-orange requirement and quite vocal about it.
He yelled, "If I didn't have that damned orange hat on, this
wouldn't have ever happened!"

John spent two years slowly putting the pieces together
regarding this shooting, finally pinpointing the man who
had committed the crime. The man who fired the shot said
he'd be willing to confess in front of me but not in front of
John because he was too embarrassed to admit his guilt in
front of the warden he had befriended.

Back in the seventies, the law enforcement agencies in
Maine—the State Police, sheriff's deputies, game wardens,
and many others—had little use for each other. I'm not sure
why that was; it really made no sense. But John was different. Right from the start he spent time with the troopers and

sheriff's' deputies because he knew and respected the fact that we all were doing the same thing. That level of cooperation paid off for law enforcement in Waldo County. When two state prison escapees ended up in John's territory in the mid-eighties, the State Police were fully in charge of the operation, but at the morning meetings John was always at the table and was in the lead for the capture.

Throughout his career, we all knew John was keeping a diary of his adventures. Most wardens retained their daily work records, which could jog their memory about a person or place they wanted to keep an eye on. But I'm sure John's were more copious and quite funny as well. As I look back upon it, I think the comedy was kind of a cover-up for the many stresses associated with being a game warden. I'm sure it was a great release for him—and I know it was for those of us who heard and enjoyed his many stories.

I understand John has included me in some of these stories. He'd better be extremely careful because I've got some really good ones about him, too, as do many of his peers.

John Marsh
February 2011

John Marsh was the Chief Warden of Maine from 1982 to 1988. He supervised 125 uniformed men and helped make significant policy decisions, including Maine's first moose hunt. He also helped organize Maine's search-and-rescue squads, which are now a national model. He served three terms in the Maine Legislature after his retirement. He lives in West Gardiner with his wife Judy, who still misses the presence of wardens in her life.

Introduction

I joined the Maine Warden Service in September of 1970, fulfilling a childhood dream of one day following in the footsteps of my family members by pursuing a career in law enforcement. Most of my family had been involved in law enforcement in one way or another over the years.

My grandfather, Leland Ford, was a Maine State trooper in the earlier days of the Maine State Police. He was stationed at Troop A, patrolling the southern Maine towns around Sanford until his untimely death from pneumonia in 1954.

My father, Velmore Ford, was a part-time deputy for the York County Sheriff's Office. He, too, patrolled the Sanford-Springvale area.

My mother, Ethelind Walker, spent countless hours rehabilitating a variety of wildlife for the Department of Inland Fish and Game. Being constantly around nearly every type of wild critter imaginable piqued my interest of one day becoming a Maine Game Warden. Raccoons, fishers, otters, bobcats, deer, hawks, owls, squirrels, ducks, and several other species of game roamed throughout my yard, and my decision to pursue a career in wildlife was more determined with each new critter that came along.

We lived in Emery's Mills, a small community a few miles north of Sanford. Our house was near the shores of Mousam Lake. With swimming and fishing in the summer and skating and ice-fishing in the winter, it was a great place to grow up. There was always something to do out of doors, and the area was well noted for hunting. My brother Jerrold and I always found some means of mischief to keep us occupied.

My stepfather, Warden Vernon Walker, patrolled the Sanford-Springvale area for twenty-three years before he retired. I tagged along with Verne every chance I could get. He was the single biggest influence in my young life as to wanting to follow in his footsteps.

At an early age I was well acquainted with many of the wardens in southern Maine. The rapport and respect these men had developed with the public they served was second to none. Their mission to protect and preserve the great wildlife resources of our state seemed like a desirable ambition to pursue. Never knowing what might happen from one moment to the next was also exciting for a young fellow still unsure of what his destiny in life might be.

I struggled through Sanford High School, graduating as a medium student at best. I couldn't seem to put forth any extra effort to get the most out of my studies. I'd much rather be off hiking in the woods or fishing out on the pond. I was unable to correlate the importance of school-work in reference to the dream I was pursuing. I intended on becoming a Maine Game Warden come hell or high water, and geometry, algebra, chemistry, and the like certainly weren't going to make any difference whatsoever—or so I thought.

The only subject I excelled in was art. And even then, I only drew wildlife scenes or painted landscapes of a remote trout brook or other rural locations I envisioned. I did create one portrait, however, a not-too-pretty caricature of my chemistry teacher. I didn't particularly care for the man and I simply hated and never understood chemistry. He caught me in the act as I sat in the back row of his class. In a fit of sheer rage he ordered me to bring my artistic rendition up to the front of the classroom for the entire class to view.

It wasn't a very complimentary portrait by any means. I regretted drawing it, and I'm sure the teacher later regretted having me show it. But his demand was met, resulting in a quick trip to the principal's office and my very last day of chemistry forever. That drawing was nearly my undoing for graduating. (Incidentally, the principal confided that he could see a close resemblance to my chemistry teacher in the drawing.)

One year of working in a plastics factory in Sanford after high school was more than I could stand. Never being able to look outside from within the dark factory walls took its toll. I decided that it was time to see the world while I was young and single. I ventured into the Air Force recruiter's office and made a four-year commitment to Uncle Sam, much to my folks' chagrin.

After basic training I volunteered for duties in Vietnam and Alaska and was thoroughly surprised when I was to sent back to Maine instead, as a radar operator at a small air base in Topsham. So much for seeing the world. While there, I took the written warden exam and passed with flying colors, but I still had a few years to go before completing my military obligation.

Courtesy of John Ford Sr.

Maine Game Warden John Ford Sr.

A week after my discharge, I was called to Fish and Game headquarters for a chief warden's interview and an oral board exam. On September 20, 1970, I was sworn in as one of the newest members of the elite team of wardens covering the state. The pay was a whopping $70 a week for 120 hours of work, six days on and two off, except for the fall when all days off were canceled. Oh, and I was to be on call twenty-four hours a day.

I was proud and excited. My childhood dreams had become reality and my adventures were about to begin. I would have what I could only consider a front-row seat to life itself.

Burnham, northeast of Waterville, was my destination. I picked up my supplies in Augusta and headed north for that paradise and some of the best deer-hunting country in the state.

Verne Walker wisely advised this rookie warden to maintain a daily diary of moments I enjoyed most during my career. "You'll forget what you did two days ago if you don't. Take it from one who knows," he said with a chuckle. "Who knows—maybe someday you can write a book about your own adventures."

My mentor also gave me another bit of advice that I treasured and have always tried to follow: "John, you treat those folks the same way you'd like to be treated and you'll get their respect. Be firm, but more so, be fair. And remember, they shot deer illegally up in that gawd-damned country long before you arrived on the scene, and they sure as hell will be shooting them illegally long after you're gone. Just be firm and fair, and you'll do just fine."

Great advice from a great man.

I've enjoyed my front-row seat to life. I got to see the very best of my neighbors, and at times, the very worst. The twenty years flew by like it was only yesterday, and never for one minute did it feel like work. It has been a journey I truly feel I was blessed to have taken, and I have no regrets. Sportsmen of Maine are by far the very best anywhere, and the many friends I made along the way will remain as friends forever—even those I found myself holding accountable every now and then.

Over the years, thanks to Verne, I recorded my adventures, mostly the humorous ones of my own doing and demise, more so than the tragic incidents. I share some of them here with you now, with some of the subjects' names changed to protect their privacy. I hope you enjoy the trip.

John Ford Sr.
April 2012

Just Dropping In, Ladies

As a new warden, I was desperately trying to learn the geography and the layout of my unfamiliar district. So when Warden Pilot Richard Varney offered to take me along in his plane for an aerial view, I said sure.

Dick was a veteran pilot from Readfield and his personality was second to none. The floatplane circled low over the treetops and dropped down onto Unity Pond where it gracefully floated toward me. With a mighty roar of the engine, Dick maneuvered the aircraft to the boat ramp and I climbed aboard.

Once inside, Dick and I exchanged cordial greetings. I tightened the seat belt around my scrawny body. The engine roared again as the plane took off across the lake, picking up speed as we moved along. In no time we abruptly lifted off, rising up into the heavens, leaving the water and land far below us.

I marveled at the great career I had chosen. After all, in what other profession could a rookie summon an airplane at his whim, cruise over the countryside below, and get paid for doing it?

At an altitude of a couple thousand feet, Dick leveled the plane and we began charting the land below us using the topographical maps spread out between the seats. We struggled to find out exactly where we were as Dick had very little experience flying over this area, and I had none.

We circled and banked, swooped down for a closer view, and then climbed back up into the air for a different outlook, searching for landmarks I could recognize.

The steady drone of the engine, along with the constant dipping up and down, banking sharply around one area and then moving to another, was beginning to take its toll. Suddenly, I wasn't feeling all that well.

Dick noticed my flushed face and how I wasn't looking down but kept staring straight ahead. The fact that I was no longer communicating with him sealed the prognosis that his passenger wasn't quite as healthy as he had been.

We were approaching the northern end of Unity Pond when he said, "Hey, John, there's a couple of people fishing out of a canoe down on the pond. Do you want to drop down and check their licenses and perhaps get a little fresh air?"

I felt as though I was about ready to vomit and I just wanted to land, period. I nodded my approval for him to set the flying beast down. The sooner the better, I thought.

Dick settled the plane down over the pond with a thud, the pontoons striking the water's surface and slowing us to a mere crawl. He opened the windows of the aircraft, allowing a gush of fresh air into the cockpit. Believe me, by now I fully understood what that old saying "a breath of fresh air" really meant.

I welcomed the cool wind as we taxied across the water, heading for two women fishing from their canoe. They were in a secluded cove, out of sight from the main lake.

Looking forward to an opportunity to move about, I opened the door of the aircraft and unhooked the safety belts holding me firmly in place. At the same time, I repositioned the seat to make it easier to get out of the plane.

Screwing my warden's hat securely on my head, I suavely jumped down toward the pontoon. The problem was, I didn't come close to landing on it. Instead, I shot straight down into the water and completely out of sight.

There was no way in the hinges of hell that I wanted to resurface from the bottom of the pond. I could only imagine the fiasco this incident was about to become.

It was a matter of sheer survival that forced me to finally bob back up to the top, where my warden's hat floated directly above me. I scrambled onto the pontoon, grabbing my hat along the way. There I stood, with water pouring out of my holster and dripping off my head, exposed for the whole world around me to admire. I had to have looked like a drowned duck in a swamp.

All I could hear was Dick's hysterical laughter coming from inside the plane. Glancing over at the two ladies in the canoe, one of them was pinching her lips, desperately trying to maintain some form of composure. The other lady had already lost hers. She was howling in a fit of laughter.

How would I explain this embarrassing feat in front of two members of the public I'd never met before?

I knew I had to say something to break the ice, so I made it sound like I'd planned such a grand entrance. I glanced toward Dick and sputtered, "I guess they're legal, Dick; I didn't see any hidden stringer of fish beneath their canoe!"

My stupid statement enhanced their humor all the more. By now, all three of them were having a great belly laugh.

And they were having it at my sorry expense. I could only laugh along with them.

After a quick check of their licenses and an apology for ruining their fishing excursion, Dick and I floated away from the scene of this catastrophe. Rather humbly I told my still-hysterical comrade, "I think I've had quite enough flying for today, Dick. You'd better take me back to my cruiser." Between chuckles, he said, "I'd say you have, John! I promise no one will ever hear about this . . . ha-ha-ha."

I knew damn well it would only be a matter of hours before the story of our day together would be told around the state. I wasn't disappointed.

As a sad footnote to this now-humorous memory, two years later Warden Varney lost his life on Maranacook Lake in the town of Winthrop when the helicopter he was piloting malfunctioned and plunged into the water. Tragically, Dick, who was unable to swim, drowned in the incident.

I still think of that day out on Unity Pond, when I saw my friend share a moment of sheer laughter, even if it was at my expense. I'm sure it was one of the more humorous memories he ever experienced during his long career with the agency. I just wish it hadn't been about me.

Caught in the Trap

My old pal Curly had his trapping rights suspended for a year. I doubted this would curtail his efforts: Though he was a likable fellow, Curly had a stubborn streak when it came to fish and game matters, and he wasn't alone in that line of thinking. Maine had more than its fair share of folks who felt the same way, and we wardens spent countless hours tracking them down.

I realized, however, if it weren't for them, I wouldn't have a job. With that in mind, I refused to take their activities personally, and I hoped the feeling was mutual.

The exorbitant price of furs was way too high for someone skilled at the trade to not pursue the activity vigorously. Curly was definitely skilled as a trapper, far more than I happened to be. I knew Curly well enough to realize that if he figured he could get away with it, he'd be trapping just as he had in the past, suspended or not.

So I decided to check a remote area in Thorndike near Curly's home, a place where he had trapped in the past. As I hiked out through the woods, I found several dead chickens tacked to the base of trees, a well-known ploy to draw fishers into the area. I expected that within a few days, traps would be placed at the base of these baited trees, though it was still a few weeks before the start of trapping season.

I suspected Curly was the culprit. The fact that his license had been suspended gave my surveillance an extra kick. Over the next few days I regularly checked the area, but found nothing illegal. It was clear fishers were responding to the bait, though, so it was only a matter of time before the traps would appear.

The season was due to officially open on October 28. At three o'clock that morning I hid my cruiser far away from the area and headed into the woods. I'd brought along plenty of snacks and a book to read.

At daybreak I was comfortably snuggled in among the bushes, from which I could see the tote road where I expected I'd see Curly diddley-bopping along with a handful of traps, thinking he was all alone out here in the big wide world.

About eight o'clock I heard the crunching of brush and the quiet purr of an engine slowly heading my way. Sure enough, it was my pal Curly's car. This was going to be way too easy, I chuckled to myself.

I slid underneath a low-hanging hemlock tree for cover as the car stopped a short distance away. Much to my amazement, Curly wasn't in it. Instead, I watched as his wife, Fay, and her friend, Leona, opened the back of the station wagon, removed a small wooden box, and then headed out toward where one of the dead chickens had been tacked.

Surely, I thought to myself, these women wouldn't be setting traps? Around here, women weren't noted for being trappers. But what else could they be doing? I waited until they returned to the car, replaced the wooden box, and continued on down the road.

These ladies had done nothing illegal, so I didn't want to let them know the eyes of the law were watching them. I waited until they were well out of sight before I hiked over to where the chicken had been preset to see if anything had changed.

This is where my own stupidity comes into play.

At the base of the tree, a fresh chicken had replaced the old one. There was a small mound of freshly sifted dirt on the ground. Without thinking, I bent down and began to brush the silt away with my hand.

Suddenly—*ka-snap*—the jaws of a metal trap firmly latched onto my right paw. It hurt like hell and I jumped back with the trap firmly clamped on the ends of my throbbing fingers.

I wanted to swear, but I knew if I did the women would hear me. I spent the next few minutes prying the metal jaws apart, slowly removing one finger at a time, making sure each of them still functioned properly.

Eventually, I freed myself. I couldn't help but laugh at how stupid I'd been for putting myself in such a predicament. Then I stood back, dumbfounded, in total disbelief that Fay and Leona were actually trapping. It was a definite first for me.

My evil mind had falsely accused Curly. I learned a valuable lesson the hard way that cool fall morning: Sometimes the mind can convince us of things that aren't always what we think they are. This was one of those times.

Another lesson I learned from this foolish escapade was to never doubt a sportsman's wife in regards to her outdoor capabilities. It's a losing proposition. Over the next few days, my throbbing fingers and sore paw could properly vouch for this fact.

Drop the Waders!

Every spring near the end of March or early April, fishermen anxiously awaited the moment when the ice would depart the lake and the frogs would come out of hibernation so they could once again gather at Bither Brook in Unity to share an evening of heavy drinking while capturing a mess of smelts to take home to the family. It was a seasonal ritual, a time when they could get themselves outside away from Momma and the kids and share some quality time with their neighbors at the brook well after dark.

Most of the time these men gathered in a tight circle around a bonfire, passing around jugs of home brew and other liquid spirits while enjoying the camaraderie of friends. There was no doubt this was the highlight of the season for many of them.

I found myself being indoctrinated into the event in a manner that, more than likely under today's working conditions and rules, would have been an actionable offense—I'd have been fired. However, there was some good to come out of my first adventure at the little rural brook. One night's eagerness to be one of the gang somehow managed to gain a little mutual respect from those who were among the regular attendees.

I wanted to make my presence known, seeing as I was what Arthur, the nightly overseer of the booze and bonfire detail, called an "old *repubate* and the area's newest fish-cop." Arthur was well known for poaching abilities. Matter of fact, he was the recipient of the very first summons I issued after assuming my official duties in the area, so we were on a first-name basis. It was the rest of the gang gathered around the bonfire that I had yet to meet. I'd been told by my old warden friend, Milt Scribner, that most of them needed watching. Given the opportunity, they'd clean the brook out of every smelt swimming upstream to spawn.

The festivities were going full scale when I sidled in among them. The joke-telling was constant, boisterous laughter echoed throughout the wooded area, and the jug of home brew continued making its rounds, until it got to me. Up until that time, hardly anyone had noticed me.

"John, you gawd-damned old repubate you! Welcome aboard," Arthur said. He introduced me to the group, making sure to be loud enough so that those fishermen who were after smelts in the nearby stream could hear.

The jug was thrust into my hands and there was dead silence as everyone waited to see whether I'd partake. Wanting to make them think I was one of them, I tipped the jug up to my lips and took a large sip of Arthur's specialty. I had to admit, it certainly warmed my innards. The gang nodded their approval and I handed the jug on down the line. I had passed muster.

The storytelling and laughter resumed. Eventually, I even found myself telling a few raunchy stories of my own, much to the delight of the crowd, which by now was thinning a little. It seemed as though that jug of Arthur's brew kept returning to me awful quickly.

I awoke the next morning on my couch with my pants half on and half off. Not having a clue as to how I got there, I only could wonder how many smelts left the brook the night before, well over the legal limit of four quarts. All I did know was that my head ached as if someone had smashed me between the eyes with a sledgehammer.

Later, I learned that the Bither Brook gang had decided I was an all-right dude, after all, so I guess that was worth my headache. But from that day forward I vowed to pass the jug along should I find myself standing around the bonfire with those guys again. And soon, there I was.

A couple of my new cronies told me about one fisherman, Dave, who was taking well over his limit of smelts from the brook. Nearly every fisherman wore a pair of chest-waders so they could venture out into the deep water. Dave, apparently, after filling his containers to the brim with the legal limit of fish, would then fill his chest-waders with many more. In the past, I'd checked his catch as he was leaving the area, none the wiser about his blatant abuse of the rules.

"The stupid #$@%*& doesn't have a clue of what's going on. I can walk right past him with way over my daily limit," he chirped to his so-called buddies about me, the numb, new, baby game warden.

His arrogance apparently was a little more than some of the gang could put up with, so they told me. It was quite obvious they wanted to teach their comrade a lesson and they hoped I'd do my part.

A few nights later, Dave was back at the brook. I closely watched his every move, especially since there was a terrific run of smelt that night. As the evening wore on, he headed upstream well away from the glow of the bonfire and the

17

other fishermen. After a few glances around him, he pulled the top of his waders out and emptied several nets full of fish inside them. He tugged and pulled at the rubber suit to allow the smelts to settle down around his midsection and legs.

He made his way back to the rest of us, bragging as usual that he'd caught yet another good limit of smelts to clean and fry. "Time to go home," he said.

With parting winks and grins from a few of the men gathered around the fire, I tagged along a short distance behind him.

At the parking lot, I caught up with Dave and asked him if I could check his limit of smelts.

"Sure you can! I got my usual limit, John," he answered calmly, acting as if I was his long-lost buddy.

"Damn, you've done well, Dave. It's great to see how successful you are night after night," I said. "I'll just measure them to make sure you don't have too many. I want to treat everybody the same. The boss will give me hell if I don't."

"Yup, no problem, John," Dave said. "You're only doing your job."

"That's right, that's exactly what I'm doing. I really appreciate your cooperation."

I slowly measured out the legal limit of fish he was allowed to keep.

"I guess I'm all set, huh, John?"

"I reckon you are, Dave, but can I ask you an honest question?"

"Sure, what's that?"

"Dave, I've heard through the grapevine that some fishermen are leaving here, night after night, with their waders stuffed right full of smelts after they've reached their legal limit. Can you imagine anyone doing something like that?"

I watched a heavy bead of sweat appear on Dave's forehead. He stuttered, "You gotta be kidding me, John! Who to hell would ever think of doing such a thing?"

Before I could respond, he blurted, "But you know, John, it's funny you should mention it, because in the past I've found a couple of smelts that accidentally fell into my waders. They had to have fallen out of the net while I was filling my containers."

"I suppose it's possible," I said, "but I think that would be quite a rare possibility, highly improbable!"

By now, beads of sweat were streaming down Dave's forehead. His hands were trembling and he didn't seem to be quite the usual calm, self-assured person he was a few minutes before.

"Dave, you wouldn't mind dropping your waders to see if possibly a few might have slipped inside tonight, would you? I'm going to be checking everybody just to see how rare the chances of these fish falling into their waders might be."

He hesitated before saying he would, then he started lowering the rubber waders. Smelts began falling all over the ground. Some stuck to his clothes.

"Well, I'll be damned! I must've missed my bu-bu-bucket more than I th-th-thought," he sputtered, as the fish kept falling away from his rubber suit.

A few moments passed before he said, "You don't believe any of that, do you, John?"

"To be honest, Dave, no, I guess I really don't."

"I guess you got me then. I should have known better! Who told on me?"

"Yeah, Dave, you really should have known better! And as far as who told on you, what makes you think that some-one did?" I asked him this while handing him an invitation to appear before the judge.

I couldn't resist. "You know something else, Dave?"

"What's that?" he sheepishly mumbled.

"Someone once told me that even a big old fish would never have gotten caught if only he'd kept his big mouth shut."

He knew what I meant.

Before Dave left that night, he pulled me aside. "Can I let you in on a little secret, John, just between you and me?" he asked. "Did you know that Arthur is getting more than his fair share of smelts down here, night after night? He watches you like a hawk, and then he stashes buckets of extra smelts out near the road. He comes back in the wee morning hours to get them after he knows you've gone home. I'd love to see him get caught!"

And so it was along the shores of Unity Pond on those cold spring nights. I learned there is no honor among poachers. Whenever the chips are down for one, it's reward-ing for them to put someone else in the same boat. I sup-pose it's their means of justifying their own devious actions by telling on others who are doing the same thing.

Life was good at the smelt brook, and it appeared my job was getting easier with each passing season. The bonfire gang certainly provided me with a fair share of entertain-ment over the years. It was a good time for sure.

A Master Manure-Spreader Gets His Comeuppance

Waldo County is well known for having an abundance of deer and an absence of money. So when a man I'll call Larry began remodeling an old sporting camp into a first-class magnet for well-off hunters, my ears perked up.

Larry invested a small fortune on the shores of Unity Pond. He built a new lodge out of large logs, complete with a huge fireplace, a new kitchen and dining room, and a well-stocked bar for the evenings' entertainment.

Come fall, Larry hosted a steak and lobster feed at the facility, inviting several state dignitaries and all the top brass at the Fish and Game Department, including the commissioner. I, a lowly warden, was on the guest list, too, along with my colleague, Lowell Thomas.

Larry also included noted sportswriters Bud Leavitt from the *Bangor Daily News* and Gene Letourneau from the Guy Gannett Publishing Co. to join the festivities. A smart move on his part, as the two journalists gave him a tremendous amount of free "attaboys" in their articles, lavishly praising the new facility, all for the price of a few steaks and lobsters.

Living nearby, I became acquainted with Larry while he was constructing the hideaway. I wanted to be excited about the project, especially because Larry, a Registered Maine Guide, spoke of a strong commitment to operating a respectable establishment, and he endlessly promoted the entire region for its abundance of wildlife.

But for some reason, I was skeptical of Larry's sincerity about the venture. I was uncomfortable with anyone who insisted on calling me Mr. Ford instead of John, as I preferred. I was of the impression that Larry was too polite and sticky-sweet to be genuine. But I wasn't about to tell anyone about my concerns without something to justify my gut feelings.

When the hunting season began, Larry recruited several local Maine Guides, men whose reputations weren't squeaky-clean by any stretch of the imagination. These guides were quite active during the hunting season, ferrying clients to prime hunting locations and keeping them entertained, well fed, and happy. That's what the business was all about.

Right from the get-go I began hearing rumors of illegal activities at the camp. Supposedly, every night there was an excessive amount of drinking and partying at the main lodge, hardly a rarity at a Maine hunting camp. But it didn't stop there.

I had an inside informant who told me Larry would brag, "I know the gawd-damned game warden up the road—and he's no threat to anything we do."

If what my informant was telling me was true, at least my doubts were confirmed. I simply filed the information away, planning to dedicate a little more patrol effort toward the camp's hunters.

That first year, I managed to cite a few of Larry's clients for minor violations. It never failed that, whenever I issued a

summons to one of his guests, Larry would pay me an immediate visit, humbly apologizing for the infraction and assur-
ing me it would never happen again.

Yeah, yeah, yeah, I thought as he'd ramble on, and I'm
sure the sun will never rise in the east again.

I was definitely being bullshitted by a master manure-
spreader, and I knew it. But still I managed to maintain a
pleasant smile and friendly attitude, letting Larry believe I
was swallowing every phony word he managed to utter.

Then, the State Police asked me to assist them in monitoring the activities of a group of Rhode Island Mafia bosses
who had supposedly booked a hunt at Larry's lodge. They
asked me to keep a log on these suspect hunters and to note
license plates and other pertinent information.

The police captain was quick to point out, "If you should
catch any of them in a bad position, it's doubtful they'll give
you a hard time. They'll be extremely polite and more than
likely offer to pay their fines without controversy. The last
thing they want is to bring attention to themselves in a way
that might cause them grief in our state."

The very next day, one of these men was cited for a
hunting violation, and just as the captain had said, he was
extremely cooperative and congenial, offering to pay his
fine on the spot. He was told instead to contact the court in
Belfast and pay the fine directly through a guilty waiver,
which he did. There was no doubt these guys surely didn't
want another group of officers breathing down their necks.

As usual, the violation brought a visit from Larry. "Mr.
Ford, I want to apologize for my sport's actions," he began.
"I gave them boys hell up one side and down the other,
advising them we run a good ship here and we don't want it

23

ruined because of their disregard for the fish and game rules."

I pretended he was sincere and accepted his apology, all the while thinking: The shit-spreader has just gone into high gear; it's time to take a shower to wash off the filth.

In time, my informant told me that Larry was offering trophy bucks to his hunters when they departed camp. Whether the hunter shot it himself or not didn't matter. For a hefty fee, every hunter was guaranteed a deer to take home.

Such a practice was highly illegal. Moreover, it was highly unprofessional, especially for a Maine Guide and the proprietor of a sporting camp. But as before, these accusations were word-of-mouth from an inside source, and I'd need solid evidence if I was to bring charges.

At the end of the hunting season, I sought the assistance of the department's undercover investigators. I told them about the many rumors I'd heard from someone inside the outfit, who was deathly afraid of being exposed.

Two of the best undercover agents at Fish and Game were assigned the case. Late the next summer, posing as nonresident fishermen, they booked a few days at the camp, a great chance to become acquainted with the owner and check out his operation.

These agents were extremely good at what they did. In the evening they swapped stories and shared drinks with their host and his guides inside the swanky lodge. Their easygoing demeanor and flagrant displays of money quickly caught the attention of those around them.

They discussed making reservations to come back in the fall for a hunt. Larry assured them they'd definitely enjoy it, and indicated they could each leave with a trophy should they follow through with their plan.

Assurances of a deer to take home wasn't an outright guarantee by Larry, but it certainly was enough for the undercover wardens to return to the lodge in the fall.

Come November, the wardens arrived at the camp as scheduled. During the first night of sharing drinks with Larry and the crew, they again were assured they'd have a deer to take home when they left. The price could be negotiated, but it might cost them a little more for a good trophy buck.

Larry suggested a host of activities to keep them entertained during their stay, including some that were not quite legal.

"What about the game wardens—aren't you afraid they'll catch you guys?" the investigators inquired. Not to worry, said their host. "I know where Old John Boy is most of the time, and I'm certainly not intimidated by him."

That first year that the wardens infiltrated the sporting camp was quite productive. They were able to document a variety of illegal activities by Larry and his crew. However, because of another obligation, they had to depart the camp before they could prove that illegal deer marketing was being offered there. We met at the end of the hunting season and decided to try again the next year.

The following fall, the two investigators arrived at the camp, where they were viewed as old pals. They were wined and dined right straight ahead, partying every night with the louts they were investigating and learning more and more about the sporting camp's deceitful practices.

The agents were offered the opportunity to go on a night-hunting excursion by canoe along the banks of the

Sebasticook River between the towns of Burnham and
Clinton. The guides said they would scan the riverbanks
with their bright flashlights in areas heavily baited with
apples, making the deer easy prey to a well-placed charge of
buckshot. Prior excursions always netted a big buck or two,
they said.

Describing the trip, Larry held a large steel flashlight
high over his head, loudly proclaiming, "And this is for my
little buddy up the road, should the son of a bitch try to
stop us." The wardens took his gesture as a threat to resort
to violence if someone—me—attempted to meddle.

During the nightly drinking sessions, my name was frequently mentioned, along with a few other wardens in the
area, the undercover wardens told me. Larry and his crew
bragged about how blind we were to their illegal activities.
If only they knew. There was a day of reckoning coming—
and I couldn't wait.

A prime example of the corruption running amok at this
camp occurred one evening during a torrential downpour,
heavy wind, and occasional lightning. One of Larry's sports
was missing, apparently having gotten lost after leaving a
tree stand that afternoon.

The worried hunters, fearing something bad might have
happened to their friend, suggested to Larry and his crew
that they should notify the local warden to organize a
search. By then Larry and his guides were pretty well intoxi-
cated, as was customary for that hour of the night. They
were adamant that "they didn't want the gawd-damned game
wardens involved, especially the one up the road." However,
after trying to locate the hunter on their own for several
hours, they finally decided to seek help.

It was nearly eight o'clock when I arrived. Trying to gather information from this group was like trying to pull eyeteeth out of a tiger. Their drunkenness and dislike for anyone in uniform was quite obvious. My strategy of remaining courteous and polite to these men had ended as far as I was concerned.

Two of Larry's guides said they would head over to a road that paralleled the area being searched, where they'd fire a couple of shots into the air, hoping the missing hunter would hear them. Instead of going where they said, though, the two men drove to South Unity knowing that I, out on the search some distance away, wouldn't be any threat to their illegal actions.

They shot a large buck underneath their headlights. Scooping up the carcass, they scurried back to the sporting camp, placing the buck out of sight to be dressed off later. Then they went to the search site and nonchalantly said they didn't have any luck contacting the missing hunter.

Finally, the missing hunter emerged from the woods on his own, quite some distance from where we had been searching.

Larry's crew hustled the cold, wet, and hungry man back to the lodge to continue with the evening's partying. They openly boasted about taking advantage of the search, bagging one of their biggest bucks of the fall. It was even suggested that they should come up with more lost hunters so that they could repeat the evening's night-hunting success. We received absolutely no thanks for our search efforts.

The next morning, one of the undercover wardens bought the illegally harvested buck for $200. By week's end, the other warden bought a deer of his own. Instead of paying top dollar, though, he bartered and argued with the guides, finally settling on $125, much to Larry's crew's disgruntlement.

They argued, "You don't realize the chances we took to bag this critter! You're asking us to give it away!"

"Take it or leave it," the warden insisted. He knew they'd give in, having been down that road before in other transactions under similar circumstances.

The plot had thickened. At the end of the agents' stay, they had documented several illegal transactions and determined who was responsible for each one.

At the end of hunting season, the other wardens and I gathered in Belfast to decide who would be charged with what violations. We would then seek indictments from the Belfast courts and run the entire case through the prosecutor's office. It was a job well done by the two undercover agents.

A grand jury heard the case a few days before Christmas and authorized the issuance of several indictments. Once the legal work was prepared, Larry and his men received a visit from Santa Claus. Merry Christmas! Ho, ho, ho! After a two-year investigation, there was going to be sweet justice after all.

We met up with most of the men at the lodge, where, as usual, they were partaking of liquid spirits. They reacted with shock and an emphatic denial of any wrongdoing each time a summons was handed out. With a great deal of satisfaction, I was able to look them squarely in the eyes and say, "Boys, I hate to tell you this, but do you remember a couple of nonresident hunters who spent so much time with you the past two falls? Remember they ate, drank, played, and hunted with you for a long period of time? Well, guess what? They just happened to be game wardens! Just like me!

It just goes to show, you really never know who your real friends are. Do you, Larry?"

I smirked as I handed him the final indictment.

The manure-spreader had run out of anything to say, and there was a gasp between the shocked men, who now, too, were completely speechless.

The case never went to trial. The men pleaded guilty to their charges, the camp was officially put out of business, and several of its guides had their licenses revoked for a lengthy period.

Shortly afterwards, the main lodge at the sporting camp mysteriously burned in the middle of the night, and Larry's expensive misadventure became but a bad memory.

It was time for this Santa to start searching for other lawbreakers, for surely when one serious threat disappeared, another always appeared to take its place.

"If You Step in it, You'll Know"

The deer season started as it usually does. We caught a couple of night-hunters, made several arrests, and issued several summonses. In the process, we confiscated seven illegally shot deer that were now strung on the lieutenant's car, making it look like a meat wagon heading off to the slaughterhouse.

After nearly thirty straight hours of constant running, we were all completely exhausted. My colleagues, Lieutenant John Marsh and Warden Langdon Chandler, decided to call it quits. I couldn't join them as I still had one more mission to accomplish. Earlier, I'd met with a couple of young warden recruits, Jim Ross and Gary Parsons from Unity. They'd found an illegal snare in the woods out behind a hunting camp in Troy.

The camp was owned by a group of hunters from Smithfield, Rhode Island, and was situated well off the beaten path. Jim and Gary were hunting behind the camp when they came across what they described as a rope snare set on the ground, designed to capture a deer. Jim said, "You gotta see this thing, John! I've never seen anything like it before. It's a large rope-net that is spread directly across a

31

Courtesy of John Ford Sr.

Wardens John Ford, left, John Marsh, and Langdon Chandler with illegally killed deer.

deer trail, baited with apples and grain, and soaked in molasses."

Attached to the net, Jim said, were a series of ropes and pulleys connected to a couple of platforms high up in the trees. The platforms were secured on hinges and held big rocks tied with ropes connected to the net itself. When an unsuspecting deer walked into the trigger, the platforms would collapse, springing the net up around the deer and holding it captive until the trappers could get there.

I was trying to envision exactly what Jim was describing, but I couldn't seem to make a connection.

Gary chimed in, "This thing also has a series of fish lines running back to the camp through screw-eyes in the trees, alerting the hunters to any activity in the net."

"How to heck do you know that?" I inquired.

"'Cuz we set it off and they came a-running," he said. "We got the heck outta there!"

They laughed. I still couldn't picture what kind of contraption this might be, but obviously, as excited as they were, the least I could do was to check it out.

We agreed to meet at two o'clock in the morning in downtown Unity. We'd sneak in behind the camp so I could see exactly what they were talking about. I reckoned the hunters would be sound asleep, narrowing our chances of getting caught while investigating the intriguing setup.

Lieutenant Marsh and Warden Chandler were having a good time making fun of my expedition. They both assumed I was going on a wild goose chase and they were too tired to want to tag along. Instead, they were heading home to nice warm beds and some much-needed rest.

"Don't get your foot caught in that trap," the lieutenant laughed as he sped out of town.

A few hours later I'd have the last laugh.

I cuddled up inside my cruiser, grabbing a few winks of shut-eye while waiting for my faithful recruits to arrive. I'd barely gone to sleep when they were pounding on my window, anxiously anticipating the next few hours.

Not wanting to alert anyone to our presence, I parked in a gravel pit some distance from the camp. Quietly, we hiked up an old tote road, allowing our eyes to adjust to the black of night.

Before long, the silhouette of the small camp became visible, neatly tucked away in the woods with smoke pouring out the chimney. It was an extremely cold night and the wind whistled through the treetops.

There were no signs of activity inside the little hut as we crept past in stealth mode. I whispered to Gary, "Where to heck is this thing located?"

"Damned if I know," he whispered. "It all looks different in the dark. But believe me, if you step in it, you'll know."

"Great, just great! Here we are, wallowing around in the pitch of night, knowing this thing is out here somewhere, but we don't know where," I grumbled.

"Just look for the fish line coming out through the camp window. Maybe we can follow it back to the net from there," Jim piped up.

I'll be darned; the little critter is sharper than I give him credit for, I thought.

I made the boys stay well away from the camp as I sneaked up to the windows, searching for the fishing line they'd described. Lo and behold, there it was—a thin strand of monofilament coming out through a partially open window.

I started to trace it back through the woods to where Gary and Jim said the net was spread on the ground. My two cronies were following closely. "You really want to watch out, John Boy; you don't want to step into that thing," Jim warned.

A short time later we arrived at the elaborate snare, which was exactly as the boys had described. Whether it was capable of accomplishing its mission or not, who knows? It certainly had potential. I'd never heard of, or seen, anything like it.

I intended to spring the trap, hoping to draw the culprits out of the hunting camp so I could prove the illegal contraption belonged to them. If I couldn't get them to the net, they could deny any knowledge of setting the trap, and I'd be left with nothing more than a good circumstantial case.

"You guys get down over that bank over there, and you stay put until I tell you to come out. No matter what happens, be quiet until I tell you it's okay," I barked. It would've been better if I'd had the company of Marsh and Chandler, but it was too late to think about that now.

Adrenaline rushed into my veins like never before as I firmly grabbed hold of the fish line and began yanking and pulling as hard as I could. At the same time, I was loudly blatting, trying to imitate the sounds of a deer in distress.

Gary and Jim were laughing uncontrollably in the bushes. I yelled over to them as loudly as I dared, "Shut the heck up. This isn't as damned funny as you're making it out to be."

I could hear the other end of the line clanging and banging up at the camp as the hunters' alarm worked perfectly. Immediately there was a stirring of activity inside the camp. The door burst open and three beams of light came streaking down through the woods toward me.

My heart racing, I continued blatting as the lights got closer. I could barely see the silhouette of the first person bounding down the trail like a jackrabbit, though it was clear he was holding a firearm.

When they arrived at the net, I hollered, "Hold it right there, gentlemen! Hold it right there! I'm a Maine Game Warden and you're all under arrest."

The next few seconds grew quite intense as the young fellow toting the shotgun quickly raised it up to his shoulder, pointing it directly at my head. Instinctively, I pulled my department-issued .38 sidearm. We stood a few feet

Courtesy of John Ford Sr.

A fish line ran in through the camp's kitchen window, attached to a soda can filled with nuts and bolts. This served as an alarm to those inside that the trap had been sprung.

apart in a standoff. I kept screaming for him to drop the shotgun while pointing my little peashooter his way.

Then I pulled a bluff of sorts. I told them they were surrounded by other wardens, when in reality I was alone,
except for Tootie and Muldoon, aka Gary and Jim, my warden wannabees.

All three hunters were clad in pajamas. The elder member of the group finally convinced the young fellow with
the shotgun to drop it and submit to my demands. In a few
minutes they were cooperative.

I got my hands on the shotgun and escorted the group
back to the camp, preparing them for the long ride to the
Waldo County Crowbar Hotel. The camp owner, Ray, happened to be a bail bondsman from Rhode Island and knew
firsthand what the procedures were from here on in.

Ray was not the least bit upset at what had transpired.
As a matter of fact, he was quite cordial as we chatted about
deer hunting and the poor luck his camp had experienced
over these past few years. Ray pointed to a record on the
wall of his camp, noting all of the previous years' hunts. It
showed no trophy deer had ever been taken by any of the
camp's hunters.

I found this hard to believe, knowing they were hunting
in what I considered some of Maine's very best deer country.
Others who had hunted in the area had been quite successful.

Ray said, "Now you can see why we're so desperate to
try anything."

I asked him if he thought the snare would work. He
said, "I dunno. I learned how to make one of them several
years ago when I was stationed overseas in the military. We
caught a few wild critters in a net like that, but you have to
respond quickly before they get out. It was a million-in-one

shot, but after all this time of going home empty-handed, we were ready to try just about anything."

I couldn't help but think of how close my Mrs. Ford had just come to being a widow all because of a deer. A little more pressure on the trigger of that shotgun from the half-awake hunter could've tragically determined my fate.

After booking the hunters into the Waldo County Jail, I couldn't wait to make the crack-of-dawn call to Lieutenant Marsh, hopefully waking him up from a sound sleep.

His phone rang several times before I heard his groggy voice. "Hello—hello!"

"John, were you sleeping?" I sarcastically inquired.

"What the hell do you think I was doing," he stuttered, followed by a rather irritated, "What's up?"

"Well, John, I just wanted to tell you, I'm at the Waldo County Jail with three nonresident night-hunters who had an illegal deer snare. I thought you might want to know. That snare you guys were teasing me about was, in fact, the real thing."

"You're kidding me! Tell me you're kidding me," he said. I sensed he had suddenly sprung to life, seeing as how he was such a stickler for catching night-hunters. Even more, he loved to be included in the action, no matter where it was.

"What happened? Tell me what happened," he begged. I told him the hair-raising events of the past few hours while he sighed and groaned in total disgust, griping to himself for not being there.

He asked if we had taken the snare down, and I said no, not yet. He yelled, "Don't remove it!" He'd get the department photographer and head over pronto. "Damn it! Damn it! I wish I'd been there," he muttered over and over.

38

The rest of the morning was spent with Marsh, my boss, Supervisor George Nash, and a small crew of bordering wardens as we gathered up the net and photographed the entire setup.

Attached to the fish line was a soda can filled with nuts and bolts. It provided the alarm inside the camp as it banged away in a cast-iron sink under the slightly open window.

Ray and his cohorts gained the dubious distinction of being arrested for the most unusual and serious offense during the 1972 fall hunting season. After paying a record fine, they left the courthouse, shook my hand, and invited me back to their camp anytime for coffee and to chat.

"No hard feelings on this end," Ray said. "We were wrong and we knew it. You were only doing your job."

We have remained friends to this very day.

The Moody Mountain Manhunt

I can't think of a more evil pair to be loose in the woods of Waldo County than Milton Wallace and Arnold Nash. Yet there they were in midsummer of 1981, escapees from the state prison farm, one a vicious murderer convicted of sexually abusing and killing a five-year-old Freeport boy, the other a well-known burglar.

I was on a family vacation at Mousam Lake in York County, my childhood stomping grounds, when I read that Wallace and Nash had walked away from a farm detail on July 15. I was sure they'd be captured before I got back to work. Either that, or they'd be fishing in Idaho or eating rice and beans in Mexico, among the few Maine prison inmates to make good on an escape. Wrong again.

The morning of my return to duty, August 1, I read an article in a national sporting magazine about the brutal slayings a few months earlier of two Idaho game wardens, Conley Elms and Bill Pogue. These two conservation officers went into the rugged backcountry to arrest a self-proclaimed mountain man and alleged poacher by the name of Claude Dallas Jr. When confronted at his campsite, Dallas executed the two lawmen without any sign of compassion for human life. He dumped one of their bodies in a nearby river and hid the other in a coyote cave.

The magazine article emphasized for me that being a law enforcement officer is indeed a dangerous profession. You never know what evil lurks in the minds of others. Little did I realize that by day's end I'd have visions of my own demise, although under somewhat different circumstances.

On that hot August day, Dispatch advised all units of a possible sighting of the two escapees on the Muzzy Ridge Road in Searsmont, a small town of fewer than a thousand residents about twenty minutes from the coast. A landowner reported seeing two men fill a red, plastic milk crate with vegetables from her garden before heading for the woods. From the detailed description, it sounded as if the suspects were the missing inmates.

State Police Trooper Dennis Hayden with his K-9, Skipper, and I were the first officers to arrive, followed by a small battalion of police officers, deputies, and wardens. We cordoned off the area between the Muzzy Ridge and Moody Mountain roads in an attempt to keep the escapees contained.

Dennis was already winding up Skipper, preparing him to strike out on a nearby woods road next to the garden, hot on the trail of the two men. I was lumbering along behind the burly trooper and his dog, scanning the area with my shotgun in the ready position.

On a dead run, we had gone a short distance along the tote road when we came across the red milk crate in a ditch. It was obvious we were heading in the right direction, although the escapees had well over an hour's head start.

Skipper was eagerly running ahead on his leash, sniffing and working, and we desperately attempted to keep up with him. The sweat poured off us as we continued through the woods, heading straight for the Moody Mountain Road.

We could hear a host of police officers chatting over the portable radio as they came screaming into the region from every direction. Each of them played a vital role in establishing a barrier to prevent the escapees from fleeing to a paved highway and, perhaps, to freedom.

After a few hours of steady tracking and running, we arrived where the Moody Mountain Road intersected with the tote road we had been following. The trail Skipper pursued had stayed away from the road and led us directly to an old, grown-up field. We were still on the mark, as indicated by the matted grass in front of us where the two men appeared to have gone. They seemed to be sticking close to the woods, using it for cover.

We were exhausted. Skipper lay down in the tall grass, panting and puffing from the heat. We all needed a break.

We were joined by State Police Commander Sergeant James Nolan, Captain Rey Lamontagne, Colonel Alan Weeks, and other officers, all seeking whatever information we could provide.

Dennis wisely knew the limits of his dog. He told the police commanders that Skipper had done all he could for this day. He and I weren't much better off.

Lamontagne said Dennis McLellan and his K-9, Ben, would soon be along, and he asked if I wanted to work with them. "I'll be ready," I said, before draining the contents of a water bottle to replenish some of the fluids I'd lost running through the puckerbrush.

The capture of Wallace and Nash was a top priority for the Maine State Police, at the direction of then-governor Joseph Brennan. Apparently, Brennan had been the

Cumberland County district attorney when Wallace had committed his heinous crime in 1972, so it was a personal matter for the chief executive.

Warden Pilot Jim Welch was circling low in the department aircraft, attempting to spot the men from the air. If nothing else, he would hopefully keep them confined. A command post was established at the intersection of the Muzzy Ridge and Moody Mountain roads, and roadblocks were set up all around. Officers searched every vehicle and warned folks living nearby about what was going on.

It seemed impossible for these men to escape the officers who surrounded them. As the afternoon went on and the temperature rose, it was just a matter of time before we'd find where they were hiding.

Trooper McLellan finally arrived with Ben on his leash, pumped up and ready to take over where Skipper had left off. In no time, we struck out across the field, heading for the dense woods ahead.

The plane circled above and as we disappeared into the woods we could hear speakers blaring from the many police cruisers parked nearby. A short distance from where we began, McLellan said, "We're onto something here, John."

Ben was quite excited. He seemed to be concentrating most of his efforts off to our right. I held the shotgun in the ready position, not knowing what to expect as we started down a small grade along a narrow game trail that led us into even thicker brush.

McLellan whispered, "We're getting close. Ben is real excited, so keep your eyes open." You could have cut the tension in the air with a dull knife.

Suddenly, directly in front of us, from behind a thick fir tree, a voice yelled, "Drop your #$@%*& gun right now or I'll shoot!"

McLellan and I both froze. Ben was going ballistic, ready to attack, but McLellan restrained him.

I raised the shotgun to my shoulder and aimed in the direction of the voice, but all I saw was the end of a rifle barrel poking out through the thick branches. It was aimed directly at my head.

Again the voice screamed, "Drop your #$@%*& gun right now, or I'll shoot! You're covered from both directions!"

There was no way McLellan or I were about to give up our weapons. Unable to get a clear view of a target, we both jumped for cover in the bushes and landed on our stomachs a few feet from each other.

Ben furiously lunged toward the tree where the assailant was concealed. There's no question he wanted a piece of this guy and he wanted it bad. I knew at any moment we were going to be shot. I wondered how bad it was going to hurt or even if we'd feel the pain.

The article I'd read that morning about the murder of the two Idaho wardens flashed through my mind. Had this been an omen of what my day would become? My heart pounded like never before. If only I could see a target and end this bizarre predicament.

I notified the officers monitoring our efforts that we were being held at gunpoint and I provided them with directions to our location.

McLellan shouted, "I'm going to let the dog go," while the assailant continued demanding that we drop our firearms. "You're surrounded. Give it up!" he yelled. For all we knew, we could've been surrounded. We certainly had no idea where the other inmate was.

As soon as Ben was released from his leash, he bolted from McLellan's grasp and lunged for the tree at warp speed. He headed straight beneath it, bounding for his target.

A rifle shot was followed by a loud squeal. Ben pathetically dragged himself back toward his master. It was an extremely emotional sight, and I couldn't imagine how McLellan was feeling. He had raised Ben from a young pup; the dog had been a close member of his family from day one.

I made another distress call, this time advising the units posted nearby that shots had been fired and the dog had been hit. Help was promised, but we were hard to find in the thick underbrush.

McLellan carefully gathered Ben in his arms, comforting him as best he could. I continued my lookout, hoping to get a clear view of the assailants while at the same time trying to get the responding teams headed in the right direction.

Warden Jim Welch radioed that he was flying directly over us at that moment, but by the time responders looked up, the plane was already past us, and a steady stream of officers went the wrong way.

I radioed that I'd fire a shot in the air alerting the confused responders to where we were. As the exact moment I touched off the revolver, I heard footsteps coming down the trail directly behind me.

At first I thought it might be the other inmate, but instead it was my boss, Sergeant Bill Allen. He was one of a few men who actually had been headed the right way.

The instant I fired, he was rounding the bend behind us. I heard him holler, "Jees-o, Jees-o, Jees-o!" as he frantically patted himself all over and knocked his sunglasses to the ground.

After regaining his composure, he sputtered, "I knew I'd just been shot and I was looking for the #$@%*& bullet hole, wondering why to hell it didn't hurt."

Meanwhile, the two escapees had moved farther back into the thick woods. Once we were satisfied it was safe for us to move, Allen and I helped McLellan carry Ben to his cruiser for a trip to the veterinarian's office.

Since shots had been fired and the dog had been wounded, Captain Lamontagne, the officer in charge, elevated the situation to an even higher level of seriousness.

More than fifty State Police officers, as well as deputies and wardens, gathered along narrow Moody Mountain Road. Everyone was anxious to spring into action. After all, a police dog was regarded as a member of the family.

Troop Commander Lieutenant Roger Drake assembled a line of shotgun-toting officers, stationed a few feet apart, along Moody Mountain Road. The line was to push through the woods to Muzzy Ridge Road, with the hope that we'd flush the escapees toward other officers along the perimeter, or capture them along the way. It was kind of like being involved in an organized deer drive (not that I knew what that was like).

As the lieutenant relayed his instructions to the troops, a shotgun discharged at the far end of the line. Apparently, someone couldn't remember if the safety of his weapon was on or off. To be sure, the person aimed the shotgun into the air and pulled the trigger. It was definitely off and it scared the bejeezus out of those of us in the line. The lieutenant shook his head in disgust before ordering the men into the woods. "You guys stay alert and be careful now" were his parting words.

The effort was unproductive. We marched, shoulder to shoulder, through the swamp and thick woods. We easily could've walked right over the two escapees and not have known because the woods were so dense. Once again, it appeared Lady Luck was on their side.

It was late in the afternoon when everyone emerged from the woods, completing the organized drive. Meanwhile, several officers had gone door to door advising folks to evacuate their homes until the men were caught.

There was a real sense of fear in the community as residents drove past the command post leaving the area. Many had armed themselves. The entire region was cordoned off and officers were positioned close to each other along the road for the night.

Patrols constantly cruised back and forth, hoping to keep the inmates contained. The rest of us were told to go home and meet at daybreak back at the command center.

I was ready to go. It had been a long and stressful day, filled with far more excitement than I'd ever expected when I left home that morning.

During the night, one officer seated comfortably in his cruiser thought he heard footsteps heading his way. He cautiously removed his firearm, anticipating the unknown. According to rumors the next morning, the officer's revolver accidentally discharged, blowing the side window out of the police cruiser. The noise he heard turned out to be a cow in a nearby pasture. Accidents happen, and this showed just how intense the situation had become.

Another incident involved a prison guard stationed along Muzzy Ridge Road. He had to fend off a tame—yet vicious and protective—turkey. The large bird had staked out its territory and didn't want the guard sharing the spot.

When Captain Lamontagne made his rounds he found the agitated prison guard holding a large stick. When Lamontagne pulled alongside the guard to offer him a break, he asked, "What's the stick for?"

Said the guard, "You watch that gawd-damned turkey over there."

Before long, the large domestic bird, by then missing several feathers, lowered its head and charged the sentry standing in the roadway. Another short beating ensued and a small cloud of white feathers floated through the air. The turkey retreated across the street—for the moment. Standing guard in a strange area could be hazardous duty for sure.

Several more police officers, wardens, prison personnel, and their canines arrived the next morning. I once again was paired with Trooper Hayden and Skipper.

It was another extremely hot and humid day, and more than one hundred officers had assembled. They came from all over, including from neighboring states, converging on Searsmont at the request of the colonel and governor.

Late in the afternoon, after a full day of searching, Hayden loaded Skipper into the backseat of his cruiser, ready to head home. Skipper was exhausted—and so were we.

The dog blankly stared between the seats as I climbed into the car. I must've done something that he didn't like, because the next thing I knew the SOB bit the back of my uniform shirt, startling the living hell out of me—what little hell I had left, that is.

"Good boy! Good boy," Hayden commenced to praise the beast. Rewarding him for his unfriendly snap at me?

Maybe Skipper was frustrated at not being able to bite those he had been tracking and he needed a little relief. Certainly his master wasn't doing much to help the situation.

Over the next two days we continued searching, hoping there'd be a fresh sighting. There wasn't, and Captain Lamontagne was about to call off the search until there was hard evidence the escapees were still in the area. Discouraged, I headed for home.

I'd just climbed out of the shower when the phone rang. It was the captain. "John, we just had a house break on the Higgins Hill Road in Morrill. This could be them," he said. "Trooper Reitchel is en route, along with Trooper Hayden and Skipper. You've been with this from day one. Do you want to join up with them? If not, I understand," he politely offered.

"I'll grab my rain gear and be on my way," I responded.

In a torrential downpour, I headed back to the command post. We were told that a family, the Butlers, had returned home on the Higgins Hill Road a little after four-thirty in the afternoon only to find that someone had been in their house. The culprits had left food cooking on the stove and cigarettes burning in the ashtrays. Articles of wet clothing had been left behind by the intruders, who fled through a side door, scampering off into the woods when the Butlers pulled into their yard.

I met with Trooper Dick Reitchel, Captain Lamontagne, Waldo County Chief Deputy John Rainfrette, and several other officers in the Butlers' dooryard. Trooper Hayden and

Skipper arrived shortly afterwards as Reitchel was interviewing the visibly shaken owners of the small country home.

Lamontagne questioned Hayden as to whether the agency might be better off using a bloodhound to track the men rather than Skipper. Apparently, the captain was questioning whether Skipper, a German shepherd, could successfully track people in the downpour. "We're ready to go right now, Cap, just give us a chance," Hayden implored. "We'll bring 'em back, I guarantee you." Reluctantly, the captain agreed.

Skipper was primed and eager to get started as Hayden rubbed the wet clothing left behind at the Butlers' house into his face, giving him a good scent to follow. All the while, Hayden was cranking him up: "Go get 'em boy! Get the bad guys, Skip, go get 'em, boy!"

Within minutes, we headed away from the Butlers' on a dead run. We were following a narrow woods road covered with low-hanging branches as the heavy rain pelted down.

Skipper was hot on the trail. He excitedly pulled at his leash, demanding that we step up the pace. I feared the heavy rain might cause the dog to lose the scent, but he seemed to be staying right on track, tugging hard on his leash.

Hayden kept saying, "Good boy, Skip! Good boy! Go get the bad guys Skipper, get 'em, boy," as he encouraged the dog to run even faster.

The two escapees had more than an hour's head start, giving them time to seek shelter and get ready for us.

It seemed as if someone at the command post called us every five minutes on the radio to check our progress. The constant distraction was a nuisance as we desperately kept watch ahead for another ambush. In frustration, I finally turned the damned radio off.

We'd traveled a little more than a mile along the narrow road when we came upon a large bog off to our left. The trail led us out across the open meadow toward a small island in the middle of the swamp.

We were completely exposed as we hiked across the meadow. I scanned the wooded island, a few hundred yards ahead, hoping we hadn't been detected.

It was eerily quiet as we floundered through the knee-high bushes and wet grass, headed for the dry land. Hayden said, "I bet they're on that island so we want to be ready, John Boy." Skipper tugged harder at the leash.

Once on the island, Hayden made a hand gesture that we were getting close. He could tell by the way Skipper was reacting that we were about to have a confrontation. At that moment, we both saw a green raincoat draped over the low-hanging branches of a large hemlock off to our right, obviously a makeshift shelter. Skipper turned and started pouncing in that direction.

There were no signs of movement. Hayden and I separated so as not to be caught side by side, as had happened with Ben and me earlier. We cautiously neared the campsite, still a few feet away. Hayden pointed toward the shelter just as one of the men peeked out from behind the nearby trees, looking our way. He started toward the ground for what I assumed to be a gun. Hayden and I rushed toward him with our weapons drawn, screaming at the top of our lungs for him to place his hands high in the air where we could plainly see them.

Hayden had his service weapon firmly in his hand while I aimed my loaded shotgun at Milton Wallace's head and bounded through the brush, heading his way.

He continued to reach for something. I screamed, "If you don't stand to hell up right now and raise your hands toward the heavens, you're going to find your #$@%*& brains scattered all over the bushes behind you!"

I could hear Hayden making similar demands as he moved in from the opposite side of the trees. It was perfectly clear that we meant business. This time we felt we had the upper hand.

We rushed into the campsite and ordered the two escapees onto their stomachs with their arms out in front of them, as we picked up their weapons—a .22 rifle wrapped in plastic and a BB gun. Then we cuffed them. There were a few tense moments before we felt things were totally under our control. The adrenaline was pumping into our veins like a broken fire hose, spewing a rush everywhere.

Hayden held a snarling Skipper inches away from the men and shouted, "You shot this dog's buddy. I ought to give him a piece of your hide for doing that!" Skipper lunged toward them with his teeth gnashing.

It was clear to these men that at any show of resistance the dog would make bloodied slabs of hamburger out of them in a matter of seconds.

I radioed the command post: "We've got them! We've got them!"

"Where are you?" a highly excited and relieved Captain Lamontagne asked. I explained, as best I could, the shortest route to our location.

We were told to keep the two men there. The captain and Warden Lieutenant John Crabtree were headed our way to assist us in transporting them back to the command post that had been established in the Butlers' driveway.

Within what seemed like record time, Lamontagne and Crabtree, both highly excited, were bounding across the open meadow our way. It appeared as if these two commanders were racing to see who could get to the scene first. Not being prejudiced by any means, I would say that Crabtree was the first to arrive.

I vividly recall Hayden proudly shouting to his boss, "What do you think of your damn old bloodhounds now, Captain?" He had every right to make such a bold statement. Skipper had performed his duties superbly—without him, and without Ben, these men might still be on the run. I'd later learn that although there had been no structural damage when Ben was shot in the hip, his career as State Police K-9 was over.

Milton Wallace and Arnold Nash were whisked back to the Maine State Prison where they belonged. On the car ride back, Wallace said that both he and Nash were "glad the ordeal was finally over."

Along with a state trooper, I accompanied Wallace and Nash to the prison in Thomaston, where we were greeted by an obviously happy warden, Paul Vestal. "Welcome home, gentlemen," he said with a smirk as we led the men back inside the walls.

When we found them, both Wallace and Nash were scruffy, dirty, and soaked. Wallace told me he thought they were near the Canadian border, though they were just fifty miles or so from the prison. As with their dream of freedom, they came up way short of leaving the United States.

Wallace also said that after they shot Ben, they covered themselves with brush to escape detection. One of the searchers was so close to them that they saw his boots, he said.

Prison officials told me that Wallace and Nash had taken a pamphlet from the library titled, "You Alone in the Maine Woods," which I had illustrated earlier in my career. I hope that wasn't the reason they stayed free so long.

As I finally pulled into my driveway late that night, I again recalled the article involving the two Idaho game wardens, Conley Elms and Bill Pogue, who hadn't been as fortunate as me. You never know what the future has in store for you—and that's a good thing, I reckon.

More Bang for Your Buck

I received a complaint about a dead buck that floated onto a homeowner's well-manicured lawn along the banks of the Sebasticook River, a short distance from Clinton. The snowmelt had caused the river to rise drastically, and the rotting critter was beached high and dry and stunk to beat the heavens, to put it mildly.

The miserable task of removing the carcass unfortunately fell within the scope of my responsibilities. The last thing I considered was dragging the putrid-smelling beast across the lawn, loading it into the trunk of my cruiser, and riding off with it to dispose of it elsewhere. I wouldn't be able to stand the smell in my cruiser for days on end if I did, especially with my weak stomach. It would have been a nightmare.

Looking around while I considered my options, I noticed that nobody was home. I thought about simply pushing the deer back into the river and letting it float away, but I knew it would only be a matter of time before someone downstream would be calling me about the same problem—and by then it would be worse than what it already was.

Then I had a brainstorm of sorts. I remembered I had some dynamite in my trunk, left over from removing a nuisance beaver dam the day before. What better way to resolve this issue than to blow the dead critter all to hell, far out in the middle of the stream?

I ran back to the cruiser and grabbed one stick of the explosives, an electrical cap, detonating wire, and other supplies. Then I dragged the stinking carcass back into the swift current, hoping that once I placed the explosive in its chest cavity it would float away from the house to an area where I could detonate the charge. This certainly sounded practical. Unfortunately, it didn't go quite the way I hoped.

The stench from the decaying critter caused me to double over with a bad case of the dry heaves, but the job had to be done. I carved a hole in the chest cavity, and, quickly sucking in and holding a breath of fresh air in my lungs, I inserted the stick of dynamite and electrical cap deeply into the carcass.

I managed to get the beast back into the current. It ever so slowly began its journey downstream, with me feeding out the electrical wires as it moved off. The moment of truth was near.

The next thing I knew, the deer had drifted back and was caught in a whirlpool directly in the middle of the river in front of me. Around and around it went.

I began to panic, knowing what I had to do, whether I wanted to or not. Voicing the usual warning before setting off a charge of explosives, I yelled, "Dynamite! Dynamite! Dynamite!" and then connected the wires to the battery.

There was a tremendous boom, followed by a cloud of water and pieces of meat filling the sky. Instead of falling back into the river as planned, most of the buck dropped back over the complainant's lawn.

To make matters worse, the complainant had returned home just as I detonated the charge. My timing couldn't have been worse.

The homeowner, Freddy, rushed to my side, demanding to know just what the hell I thought I was doing.

Embarrassed by the carnage I'd created on his front lawn, I desperately tried to explain my reasons for proceeding as I had. I might just as well have been talking to myself. He never heard a single word I said, and it was quite obvious that no amount of talking was going to appease him. He was calling me names I hadn't heard for years—and they weren't very pretty. I feared he would assault me, but I decided perhaps I fully deserved the thumping should he choose to do so.

I spent the next two hours using Freddy's wheelbarrow and rake, picking up pieces of meat and bones from his front lawn and hauling them up the road for disposal.

I was positive my act of stupidity would generate a personnel complaint from the main office, but it never did. I almost think Freddy came to feel sorry for me as I humbly apologized to him over and over after finishing my chore of cleaning up. I doubt his damned old manicured lawn ever looked so good!

I never heard from Freddy again. I wonder why he never calls anymore.

"I'm Lost, You Know!"

On a warm August day I was assigned to assist my fellow
wardens in Newburgh, where an elderly lady with a severe
diabetic condition had wandered away from an assisted living home. The group home staff had been searching for
Marion for several hours before the warden service was notified. It was obvious they didn't want a lot of attention drawn
to their establishment, fearing the repercussions.

There was a great fear that Marion hadn't received her
required diabetes medication. Her caretakers were quick to
point out that without the medicine, she could lapse into a
potentially fatal diabetic coma.

Several of us scoured the terrain around the nursing
home, which fronted a large set of fields surrounded by
dense woods. Others checked along the roadsides, the stone
walls, and the wooded area on each side of the highway,
with no success.

Department aircraft circled overhead, scanning the
woods below for any sign of the missing Marion. Darkness
settled in and the search had to be suspended until daybreak, causing much consternation. The thought of Marion
not having her medicine was of greater concern with each

passing hour, but there was little that could be done in the darkness.

The next morning, more searchers and volunteers arrived and scoured the area, expanding outward from the nursing home as the day wore on. A National Guard helicopter flew at treetop level, at times beating the branches of thickets back so the pilot could search the forest floor below. Again, at darkness, the search was suspended. The chances of finding Marion alive and in good health were looking bleak, to say the least.

The wardens met at the command center to figure out where to search next, as we'd already gone far beyond the nursing home grounds.

On the third day, Sergeant Bill Allen and I were wandering through the woods atop a small hill, quite some distance from the home. We were discussing the fact that, by now, it was more than likely that Marion was either in a severe diabetic coma, or worse yet, she was dead. There was little doubt in our minds we were searching for an immobile body.

We heard the pounding blades of the National Guard helicopter heading close to us. Then a guardsmen shouted over the radio, "We got a glimpse of her. She is lying underneath a large pine tree a short distance from where you fellows are standing. She appears to be lying on her side and not moving."

Bill and I ran up the hill to where the noisy whirlybird was hovering. We could see Marion's motionless body on the ground in front of us, curled up in the fetal position.

We ran her way with Bill calling out, "Marion! Marion!" As we knelt down beside her, she never moved a muscle. She was motionless, on her side facing away from us. Bill gently placed his hands upon her, set to roll her over to check for a pulse or any other signs of life. I was standing behind him, ready to accept the reality that she had died.

Suddenly, she popped her eyes wide open and hollered, "I'm lost, you know!"

Needless to say, she scared the living hell out of both of us. Bill fell backward, hollering, "Jees-o, Jees-o, Jees-o!"

Neither of us could utter a sensible word.

By now, Marion was sitting up, watching us like we were a couple of Looney Tunes, which, in all probability, we were. It was a rather embarrassing moment, to say the least.

We gathered our composure, checked Marion for injuries, and asked her if she could walk.

"I can if I know where I'm going," she said. With that, we got her on her feet and led her through the woods, Bill firmly holding onto one side of her and I the other.

We brought her out to a field where a waiting pickup truck took her to the main highway. From there, she was loaded into an ambulance for a trip to Eastern Maine Medical Center in Bangor.

All things considered, Marion was none the worse for her three-day journey, other than being quite hungry, a little cold, and a bit dehydrated. She appeared to have many more years ahead of her.

As for Bill and me, we were quite a while getting over that little escapade, but at least it was one with a happy ending.

Sadly, over the years, there were far too many searches that didn't end quite so well. I often thought that many of the unhappy endings were the result of inappropriate searches that trampled clues or polluted the scent of the missing person, throwing off a searching canine.

The best advice when a person comes up missing is to immediately call the authorities. Allow them to arrive and organize a proper search before sending people off every which way without a plan.

I relied heavily upon the area's volunteer fire departments to provide the best of the manpower. These folks had a vast knowledge of the land and knew the importance of following a plan. Volunteer rescue squads were invaluable as well; in many cases they knew the missing person, as well as people in the community who might have valuable information regarding the missing person's habits. It was a help to know if it might be a case of Alzheimer's, senility, depression, or simply someone who went berry picking or hunting and lost their way. Each situation was different.

It goes without saying that Marion's "I'm lost, you know!" would be one of the most memorable endings to the scores of searches I participated in. It still brings a smile to my face whenever I think about Bill and I jumping away from her like she was a ghost rising up from the grave.

God bless you, Marion, wherever you are. You proved the point that we wardens sometimes aren't as tough as we think we are.

Last Flight into Abbott's International Airport

My career involved two activities that put my life on the line. The first one was playing with dynamite: challenging a pack of beavers for placing a damn dam where it shouldn't have been. The other was flying with Warden Dana Toothaker in the department's aircraft.

Now don't misunderstand me. As for the dynamiting, I admit I was about as experienced with explosives as a youngster trying to blow up an anthill with a conveniently placed firecracker. I didn't have a clue what the results might be, but I knew damn well before I was done I'd make a severe impact upon my intended target.

Flying, or even being around Dana Toothaker, however, was a completely different story. I just never knew what crisis we'd find ourselves in from one minute to the next. But one thing was for sure—I knew there'd be one.

Prior to becoming a pilot, Dana was considered somewhat of a "cowboy warden" by those associated with him. Fortunately for me, his district bordered mine to the south and I got to share some good quality time with the cowboy. His creativity and dedication to the job were second to none.

Back before today's elaborate snowmobile trail systems where you can cut through the woods from one end of the state to the other, we wardens spent many a winter night trying to catch snowmobilers riding on the roads or operating their unregistered snow machines illegally. Back then, many folks had little, if any, respect for the snowmobile laws that were fairly new on the books.

Driving Dana's cruiser, I would tow his idling snow machine, anchored upon a tilted trailer, while he sat proudly perched upon the seat bundled up like a penguin in a blizzard, just waiting to see a group of snowmobiles approaching in the distance.

Upon his signal, I'd come to a sudden stop and Dana would launch himself off the trailer in record time, pursuing the snow machines as they passed on by. His efforts resulted in many summonses for violators who might otherwise have easily escaped capture once they recognized the warden's cruiser.

This is just one example of what working with the "cowboy warden" was like. It was his dedication to the profession that caused my pal, Grover, a highly noted poacher in the area, to seriously despise him. I think Grover knew it would be only a matter of time before Dana would trip him up and his poaching reputation would seriously be dampened.

Riding with Dana behind the wheel in his cruiser was always like riding with Evel Knievel. Dana operated everything at one speed—wide open. I never knew when each ride might be my last, but still I found myself tagging along, completely trusting him.

Dana was promoted to department pilot shortly after I became a warden. He certainly was well qualified, having served as a fixed-wing and a helicopter pilot in Vietnam, where he earned the respect of his superiors and had the honor of flying and escorting Vice President Spiro Agnew during his tour of the war-ravaged country.

One January day in 1972, Dana and I agreed to meet for a flight up over my patrol area. Dana wanted to point out a spot in Unity Plantation where he'd witnessed several dogs roaming around, threatening the deer population. We met at the Unity Pond boat landing in the early afternoon. I watched as the small Piper Cub came sailing warp-factor eight and extremely low over the trees. Quickly he dipped down onto the frozen surface of the pond heading my way.

In a cloud of thick blowing snow, Dana maneuvered the plane to where I was eagerly waiting to climb aboard. I fastened my seat belt and away we went. We shot out across the snow-covered pond in the usual Toothaker mode. A white cloud of blowing snow behind us quickly disappeared as we hurtled straight up into the air, leaving the solid ground far below.

"Let's check the deer yards out on the Plantation," Dana shouted. "I've seen a pile of deer out there lately."

"Sounds good to me," I gulped, swallowing in a futile attempt to recover from the steep climb we'd just made.

The afternoon shadows, though, prevented us from seeing any deer. Dana had another bright idea.

"Let's fly up over Lyndon Abbott's house," he said.

Lyndon was a Maine State Police trooper and a good friend of both of us. He lived nearby in the little town of Clinton. We'd all shared many memorable moments.

"If he's home we'll just buzz his house, let him know we're around," Dana said with a snicker.

"Okay," I agreed, as if I really had any say in the matter.

The steady drone of the aircraft's engine purred away as we charted our course toward Clinton. I saw Lyndon's house off in the distance and we started our descent—heading straight for it. Lower and lower we glided as the house got bigger and bigger. We were heading on a course much lower than what I figured we should be.

Finally I yelled, "Are you gonna buzz it, Dana, or fly to hell through it?"

Courtesy of John Ford Sr.

Warden John Ford with deer that were killed by dogs.

"I think we can land in that little field behind it," Dana said with a notable amount of hesitancy. "We'll go inside for a visit and maybe even a quick cup of coffee."

I wish he'd said, "We can" rather than "I think we can." The approaching field looked extremely small to me, but he was the pilot and I trusted his judgment. Like I really had any choice otherwise.

A cluster of large white pine trees standing out like huge skyscrapers in a small city were at one end of the field. At the other end were power lines that ran next to Bellsqueeze Road. There was very little room to spare in between.

I hope to hell he knows what he's doing, I thought.

We came extremely close to striking those pines as we slowly floated down to earth, eventually touching down in the field, quickly headed for the road.

"Not a problem, John Boy," Dana loudly boasted as we taxied up to Lyndon's garage. "This baby could land on a dime and give you nine cents' change every time."

Standing outside waiting for us was Lyndon, shaking his head in total disbelief. I knew exactly what he was thinking.

We went inside and had several cups of coffee while shooting the breeze. All the while I wondered, How to hell are we going to get out of here? I didn't dare ask, though. I seriously thought about begging Lyndon for a ride back to my cruiser, but I'd be damned if I'd show Dana I was a coward.

Finally, Lyndon couldn't stand it any longer. "Dana, do you really think you can fly out of here?"

"I think so," said Dana. "I think I can rev the engine, hold the brakes, and once we round that corner, we should have plenty of room to lift off," he said.

Just hearing about his elaborate plan was good enough reason for me to make yet another bathroom run. I was seriously reconsidering begging Lyndon for that ride home.

The moment of truth finally arrived as Dana and I climbed back into the plane. Dana readied the beast for our flight out of the small field, which we had since dubbed "Abbott's International." I secured the lap belt so tight around my waist I could barely breathe.

The engine roared, followed by a huge cloud of snow blowing out behind the plane, and we shot down the narrow strip and up into the air. The trees were getting closer and closer, but it didn't matter, as we were at a point of no return. The cheeks of my you-know-what were Super-Glued onto the seat of that little aircraft. Nothing short of dynamite would have removed me, except, of course, a violent collision with a non-movable object, such as a huge pine tree.

Suddenly, the little bird shot high into the air, clearing the pine branches by mere inches. I swear I heard the branches hitting the bottom of the skis as we shot on by them.

I could breathe again. Of course, Dana had to make yet one more low-level pass over Lyndon's house to signal our success before moving on.

"Now I'll show you where I saw those dogs the other day," he said, and soon we were banking and circling over Unity Plantation at about 1,500 feet with nothing but thick woods and a frozen bog beneath us.

With little warning, the engine started sputtering and seemed to be shutting down.

I yelled, "What the hell's going on now, Dana?"

"We're about out of gas on the right tank, but the left one should be picking up any second," he said.

Meanwhile, we were rapidly descending and the engine by now was all but completely silent.

I watched the ground coming up to meet us at an alarming rate. It was obvious there was no place to land but into the trees beneath us.

Cough-cough, putt-putt, the engine shook and sputtered, and suddenly it started purring once again. We were climbing back up into the air. I sensed Dana was somewhat relieved. I was reasonably sure I'd just soiled my britches.

One close call for the day was enough, but two was pushing my limit.

"Dana, I think I'm ready to go back to my cruiser," I said. "I've enjoyed just about all of the excitement I can stand for one day."

Landing safely on frozen Unity Pond, I exited the plane in what could be described as a religious and somewhat papal move. I quickly fell to my knees, kissing and blessing the ground beneath me, glad to be back on solid footing. No Pope John was I, but for the moment I felt I had truly been blessed.

A few weeks later Dana attempted yet another landing at Abbott's International. This time the conditions were quite different. Instead of the powdery snow when we had landed, a heavy crust covered the field. That caused the plane to travel much faster after it touched down.

Lyndon was in his bathroom shaving. He saw the plane speed by his bathroom window and knew it wasn't about to stop at the roadway. He watched the wings sheer off the body of the little Piper Cub after it smacked a telephone pole in front of his house.

A stunned Dana was sitting in the fuselage in the middle of the road, looking at the carnage around him. He wasn't injured, but his ego was slightly damaged, and the plane left the area on a flatbed. Abbott's International had endured its last flight, and the airstrip was officially closed.

Dana Toothaker, one of a kind, always operated on the edge. And, for whatever the reasons might have been, I often found myself seated right alongside of him.

The Warden Gets Caught

Floyd was tall and lanky and had large ears. He spoke in a deep Maine country drawl and had a strange grin that stretched from one big ear to the other. He was comical and quick-witted, and I never knew what he was up to.

He considered himself a big-time poacher. There were certainly times when he stretched the laws a little, but by no means was Floyd at the top of my own FBI (Ford's Bureau of Investigations) list.

He constantly bragged about being able to outrun game wardens, apparently referring to the one time when I actually chased him through the woods shortly after I moved into the area.

I had found a freshly killed deer covered over with brush near a number of parked vehicles belonging to hunters, I presumed, also figuring the deer was theirs. There was no tag on the critter as required by law. The tag from a hunter's license is required to be attached to the carcass to show who had killed it.

Obviously, the person who had shot this small deer was still hunting and didn't want to bother with such a legality, knowing full well that once he'd bagged a deer he was not allowed to hunt for another one.

In order to prove guilt, I'd have to watch the person actually take possession of the animal. So I hid in the nearby brush patiently waiting for the hunters to return. They did, and Floyd, ahead of the rest of them, spotted me hunkered down in the bushes.

Immediately, he hoofed it cross-country, leading me on a mini foot-chase that covered quite a bit of ground before I finally caught up to him. Floyd nervously paced back and forth as he adamantly denied having any knowledge of the hidden deer.

He stuttered and stammered, proclaiming his innocence and acting like a little kid with his hand caught inside the cookie jar. None of Floyd's hunting buddies would claim ownership of the small deer carcass, either.

Unable to prove beyond a doubt that either he or any of his party was guilty, I ended up seizing the deer without charging anyone for the crime. I gave the deer to a needy family in the area and wondered when I'd see Floyd again.

I actually took a shine to him. We established a friendly rivalry that lasted for years. Whenever we met, he'd taunt and tease me about my job and brag about his ability to outwit the law. He'd mention how he could outrun me at any time or at any place, and, in front of his cronies and anyone else who would listen to him brag, he'd challenge me to a foot race.

A few years after the initial incident, on a Saturday night, I was standing in front of the grandstand at Unity Raceway watching a few stock-car races before heading off to work for the evening. I was chatting with my friend Bob, the owner of the track, when Floyd sidled up alongside of us.

Sporting that usual ear-to-ear grin, he boasted, "Ford, you know I still can outrun you any old time I want to."

He was proud of the attention his comments were getting from the folks around us.

I responded with a smart-assed remark or two of my own, which made him smile even more.

"One of these days, Ford, we'll have to have that foot race and settle this challenge once and for all," he said, chuckling.

Without batting an eye, I looked over at Bob and said, "What do you have planned for the half-time entertainment tonight?"

"I don't have anything special tonight, John; why do you ask?"

"Well, I've got a great idea that would entertain the many people gathered here tonight. Why don't you announce over the PA system that for this evening's half-time break you're going to line up old Floyd and me on the starting line of the track so we can settle this little dispute between us once and for all. The local lawman and the notorious poacher. I bet they'd love it!"

Before Bob could respond, Floyd disappeared far back into the crowded grandstand, ducking away like a night crawler hiding from a bright light. He made sure he wasn't seen again that night.

Thank God he didn't take me up on the offer, for without a doubt, I'd have been the one doing the disappearing act.

I enjoyed catching deliberate law violators like night-hunters and real poachers. Checking fishermen to make sure they had the license and equipment they needed, on the other hand, was a job I thoroughly despised. Pity the poor guy who'd left his life preserver on the dock before heading out onto the pond.

One day on Unity Pond, every fisherman I met excitedly told about two guys trolling past them proudly displaying three huge fish on a stringer. The fish easily weighed several pounds each, but from a distance they couldn't tell what species they were.

Unity Pond wasn't noted for its huge fish by any means. It seemed unusual for anyone to have caught a monster fish in these waters, let alone three of them on the same day. I sped off on a mission, searching for these fishermen, hoping to determine what kind of fish everybody was so excited about.

Eventually, I located them at the farther end of the lake. As I came up behind them, they were proudly displaying the stringer of large fish to folks standing along the shoreline. I recognized Floyd, sporting his trademark big grin. Just knowing who it was, I knew right then and there he was up to something devious.

Sure enough, secured to the stringer alongside his boat were three huge saltwater codfish he and his buddy had caught earlier that day far out in the ocean. These fish were hardly a product of Unity Pond, but Floyd and his buddy knew damn well their exhibit would generate a great deal of excitement among the local fishermen, who couldn't tell the difference from afar. Attaboy Floyd, I said to myself.

The most classic memory I shared with Floyd, though, occurred one fall when I foolishly engaged in a bet with his brother, Burleigh. Burleigh was the proprietor of a large strawberry field situated directly behind his house. It was a small family business, open to the public for picking when the season was on. Like Floyd, Burleigh was quite a character.

76

One morning, several of the regulars were choking down breakfast and chatting at Ray's Diner in Knox, a favorite gathering spot for a little friendship and a decent meal.

Deer season was just getting under way. The conversation at the breakfast counter somehow came around to my ability to sneak up on people without being seen.

Burleigh, in a deep raspy voice, said, "By de jaysus, it would never happen to me. I would spot you long before you even knew I was around!"

I bet Burleigh a steak dinner that I could sneak past his house in the middle of the night, right down his driveway and out into his strawberry field, and swipe a large sign he displayed directing the pickers where they should go.

He was quick to take me up on the challenge, offering to give me the entire month of November to accomplish the task. If I succeeded, he would buy me the steak feed.

The bet was the talk of the restaurant for days on end. Time clicked by and I had yet to make my move.

I'd actually forgotten about the challenge until the last day in November. With my ride-along partner, Deputy Warden Scott Sienkiewicz, in tow, we had no choice but to make the trip into the field during the wee morning hours, driving without lights, and trying to be extra quiet.

It was show-and-tell time, do or die as I looked at it. There was a free steak feed in the offing.

At two-thirty in the morning I pulled into Burleigh's lower driveway without headlights, idling down along the edge of the strawberry field. Suddenly, every light in Burleigh's barn lit up, and music started blaring full blast.

I stomped on the gas, heading straight for the targeted sign at the back of the field. Scott grabbed ahold of it as we sped back around the corner, hoping to escape before Burleigh caught us.

We were a shade too late. There Burleigh sat, proudly perched in his truck with his arms folded, his shirt on inside out, sporting a huge grin on his face just like his brother Floyd.

I failed in my secret mission, caught red-handed. I knew my time at Ray's Diner over the next few days was going to include a whole lot of ribbing.

I later learned that Burleigh had spent several hours placing trip wires across his driveway, wires that, when broken, would light up his barn and automatically turn on a radio, alerting him that he had an intruder.

He knew damn well my time had expired. If he was to win his steak dinner and the respect of his cronies, he had to move at a minute's notice. And he did. He sat in his living room chair half-asleep all night long, just waiting for the moment of truth.

Burleigh's wife was relieved that this damned foolish bet was over. She complained, "Burleigh hasn't slept for better than a month, constantly jumping out of bed looking out the window, thinking you were out there."

Later, I heard Floyd was madder than a dog with rabies at Burleigh for making such a foolish bet. Floyd, who lived close by, had planned to do a little night-hunting in the area before the fall was over, but he didn't dare do so after he heard about our deal. He didn't know when it would be safe for him to venture out, wondering if that would be the time when I'd come flying in.

There was justice after all. Although it may have cost me a steak dinner, I couldn't help thinking that even though I'd failed my mission, I might have saved a little Bambi from extinction from a beam of light and a shot from Floyd's deadly rifle.

My pal Floyd passed away at home with his family surrounding him a few months afterwards. I certainly miss that big grin and listening to the many exaggerated stories he told, always enjoying the humor that accompanied each one of them.

The Bogeyman

I was afraid of the dark as a kid, remembering all too well the stories adults told us: "Be on the lookout for the bogeyman! He just might get you!"

Even though I wore a loaded firearm as a grown-up game warden, I never got over the fear that somewhere in the silent night a bogeyman was waiting to pounce. I didn't share my fears with anyone, hoping I'd eventually conquer them on my own. I knew if I was to succeed in my new job, I'd have to overcome this mental obstacle sooner rather than later. Otherwise, the next twenty years—or the next dark night—could be quite miserable.

I was sound asleep when the call came from Sally, the owner of a Burnham nursing home.

Sally's land was prime hunting ground for deer, both day and night. Right in front of her establishment was a large field where deer often congregated for a nighttime snack. It was a perfect spot for someone driving by to blast a Bambi that was standing near the roadway.

Behind the nursing home was a pasture where Sally boarded a couple of old horses. The narrow strip of land was covered with apple trees, making it a hot spot for deer as well. This pasture was next to the Mount Road, where a veritable posse of poachers was known to live.

Sally was a gruff-talking elderly lady who didn't hesitate to tell it like it was. Swearing wasn't something she was overly cautious about, so I didn't have to dilute my own vocabulary to carry on a lively conversation with her. We'd become well acquainted as I'd assumed my duties in the area, and I'd taken quite a liking to the old gal.

I picked up the phone, groggily. "Hello . . . ?"

"John, this is Sally!" I could tell she was really riled up.

"Hi, Sally. What's up?"

"Them sons-of-bitches just fired two shots out in my back pasture," she grumbled. "I think they're there now! Gawd-damn them! I've been watching several deer underneath those apple trees and them bastards will shoot every gawd-damn one of them if they can," she sputtered.

Sally was about as grumpy as I'd ever heard her. Before I could respond, she launched into another tirade. "I'm going to give you a chance to catch them first, but if you can't come up here, I've got my gawd-damned shotgun all loaded with buckshot, and I'm ready to let it fly right out through my kitchen window. Them sons-of-bitches."

Deciding I'd better get over to her place before she shot someone, I told her I'd be right up.

"I'll be pulling into your dooryard with my headlights off," I said, carefully explaining that I didn't want to forewarn anyone who might be out in the pasture. "So for cripe's sake, don't you shoot at me!"

She assured me she wouldn't, but I still had my doubts.

Hastily donning my uniform, I sped up the road the short distance to the nursing home.

I slowed to a near crawl as I pulled into Sally's place. I scanned the pasture looking for any indication that someone was there. I got out of my cruiser with my trusty flashlight gripped tightly in my hand. I didn't plan to use it unless I had to.

Sneaking along in the darkness hoping to confront the poachers, I hiked between the barn and Sally's house and climbed over the fence separating the pasture from the dooryard. It was blacker than a boot out there.

It was extremely quiet, but at 1:15 in the morning it should have been. I suspected that if someone sneezed in Unity some six miles away, I'd hear them.

As I stood in the pasture peering into the darkness, thoughts of the bogeyman flashed through my mind. I had a weird sense of someone nearby watching my every move. It made the hairs on the back of my neck rise.

I could barely see more than four feet in front of me as I slowly worked my way into the pasture. I'd walk for a short distance and then stop, checking out the emptiness. Then I'd move a little farther out, repeating the process as I crept along. After what seemed like an eternity, I finally found myself a good distance away from the nursing home and my cruiser.

As far as I could tell, I was all alone. I hadn't heard a sound, nor was there any movement. But then again, if they were night-hunters, they'd be extremely quiet themselves, being the sneaky people they are. I cautiously poked along.

Suddenly, I walked into the hind end of a sleeping horse. The startled horse snorted loudly, springing to life like a rocket fired from its launcher. The petrified animal bolted across the pasture, kicking and blowing, grunting and bellowing.

I was just as abruptly hoofing it back to the security of my cruiser like an Olympian setting the world record in the 200-meter dash. I'm not so sure but that I didn't set that record! I hurdled over the last fence post like a skilled athlete. Within seconds I was breathlessly skidding to a halt at the door of my car.

My heart was pounding wildly as I floundered against the side of the cruiser, desperately trying to get in.

Once I was safely secured in my well-lighted car, I thought to myself, Bogeyman, my arse! Tonight I bumped into the real BOGEY-MONSTER!

Obviously this wasn't the night I'd overcome my fear of the dark. Yup, I hated to admit it, but the old bogey-horse actually won the battle early that morning out behind Sally's nursing home.

And the hunters? They must have been bogeymen in Sally's own overheated imagination.

Daddy Who?

The young lady on the telephone excitedly asked, "Are you the game warden?"

"I am! What can I help you with?"

"This is the Dixmont Corner Store. We've got a little dilemma up here that requires your expert advice," she said. "A woodcutter is here with two owl eggs that fell from a tree he cut down this morning. They appear to be okay and we're wondering what to do with them."

"Good question," I mumbled. "I doubt if they'll hatch, but I suggest that maybe you wrap them in something soft and warm, and I'll come by tomorrow morning to pick them up."

I figured it would be a waste of time trying to do anything with the eggs, but making the effort would be good public relations if nothing else. I'd simply gather them up and discard them later when no one was around. After all, who would expect these eggs to be any good after tumbling onto the ground when the woodcutter felled the tree that held their nest? The chance of either egg hatching was remote at best, but I knew if I suggested destroying them the repercussions from those who felt they were helping out Mother Nature could be brutal.

"Okay, thank you ever so much," she said. "We'll wrap them up in cotton and place them on top of the popcorn machine."

I'd forgotten all about her call when early in the morning the next day the phone rang again.

"This is the Dixmont store again. You're not going to believe this, but we did exactly as you told us to and we've just watched one of the eggs hatch! I think the other one is about ready," she gushed.

"You're kidding me," I responded in total disbelief. "I'll be up soon to get them," I promised.

Now what the hell am I going to do, I wondered.

And thus my adventure of becoming papa to a pair of young owlets began.

By the time I arrived at the store, a small crowd had gathered around the popcorn machine, watching the second egg produce another baby owl. Gathering up the small box containing the homeliest creatures God had ever created, I brought the young owls home and placed a distress call to Birdsacre, a nonprofit rehabilitation organization in Ellsworth, asking for guidance.

"Don't get your hopes up that they'll survive," I was told. "They need mice, squirrels, and other food from the wild to survive. You'll need to chop the carcasses into fine pieces, leaving the hair and bones intact."

Grabbing my trusty pair of tin snips, I became a butcher of sorts. My neighbors and friends rallied to the cause. People began dropping off dead mice, squirrels, and even woodchucks on our doorstep in an effort to provide an ample supply of feed for the little owlets.

Courtesy of John Ford Sr.

John Ford raised this owl from birth, feeding it roadkill, which he'd cut into pieces with tin snips.

All this gruesome activity didn't make Mrs. Ford any too happy. She never knew what dead creature would be draped across our doorstep from one day to the next.

I spent countless hours snipping away at these carcasses, storing the remains in little plastic tubs for future use.

Tender loving care required a change in my daily patrol routine. I found myself heading home every few hours to change the hot water bottles and force-feed my new babies.

The owlets stood only a few inches tall. They had big feet, large bulging, unopened eyes, huge beaks, and no feathers covering their fragile bodies. Staggering around in their cardboard nest, they were definitely the ugly ducklings of the owl world.

When I brushed small chunks of furry meat and the remains of dead mice and other critters across their beaks, they gobbled the goodies down like candy. They grew amazingly fast, constantly demanding more food and care.

Within a few short days, a layer of white downy feathers encased their homely bodies and their bluish-gray eyes finally opened, giving them a little character. I found myself becoming quite attached to them. I named them Who-Who and Boo-Hoo.

They'd made it through the first few hectic days and now I only hoped they'd survive. The daily routine of constant feeding continued throughout the summer. Miraculously, they were turning into masterpieces of sheer beauty. As their bodies grew, their downy covering was replaced with gray and brown feathers.

We replaced the small box that was their nest with a larger one. Their daily feedings required a lot more food, but fortunately, the highway produced enough road-killed squirrels, woodchucks, and other creatures to snip apart for future meals.

Who-Who and Boo-Hoo lived in our home right along with the rest of the Ford family, until one evening as we were watching TV one of them came staggering into the living room. They'd discovered a means of escaping from their box and were exploring the big world around them.

Mrs. Ford gruffly demanded an immediate end to their free-range lifestyle. "They'll be messing all over everything, John," she said in an authoritative voice that I fully understood.

Who-Who and Boo-Hoo were transferred down to our cellar in an area where they could roam about as they pleased. They had an open view of the woods behind our house that would eventually become their home.

Their daily diet changed from whole mice to chicken necks, which I purchased in bulk at a processing plant in Belfast. They learned how to fly on their own, spending most of the time perched on a cellar beam overlooking the wilderness outdoors.

As fall approached, the time for freedom was close at hand. By now Who-Who and Boo-Hoo were a pair of handsome, mature barred owls, a far cry from that first day when I brought the ugly little creatures home.

The final challenge was to teach them how to survive on their own. I wanted to be sure they were capable of hunting for food. I loosely attached large chunks of cut-up squirrel meat to a length of monofilament fish line. I rapidly dragged the meal across the cellar floor, in the owls' plain view. Their heads bobbed up and down as they intently watched their supper scooting along the floor.

Courtesy of John Ford Sr.

One of the owls with John Ford Jr.

After a few attempts, they discovered how to fly down from their perch and strike at the moving target, devouring the moving meal in one swift attack.

The time had come to release them back into the wilderness where they belonged. Late one September afternoon, I removed the wire barrier from the cellar door, allowing the owls to freely move outside. It took a while, but eventually they worked their way to freedom, perching in a tree at the end of our porch, where they both fell asleep.

At dusk, they flew up onto the TV antenna on our roof, where once again they dozed off for another nap. They nearly caused a major traffic jam. More than one excited passerby skidded into the dooryard, screaming, "Come outside and see what the hell is perched up on your TV antenna!"

I explained the circumstances surrounding the rare sight to those strangers and friends who stopped by for a closer look. Papa Owl was quite proud of his accomplishments.

By the next morning the owls were gone.

The next day I called out to them, hoping they'd respond at least one more time. Only then did I realize what "having the kids leave the nest" really meant. I already missed them.

Suddenly, from out of the trees they flew, landing a few feet from where I stood. Their heads were bobbing up and down as they anxiously looked for yet another handout of free grub from Dad.

In the following days, the visits became less frequent, until finally they disappeared for good. I hoped they would celebrate the life they were destined for. They had survived some rather unusual circumstances, which I never thought would be possible.

The phone rang once again. "Hello, are you the game warden?" a lady's voice inquired.

"I am, ma'am; what can I help you with?"

"Well, sir, my cat just came back from the woods and she had a little ball of fur in her mouth. I think it's a baby coyote."

Here we go again. I could hardly wait.

You're Welcome, Deer

In the spring, mother deer begin the age-old process of letting their offspring go. The little ones wander through the woods, the does watching carefully as they take their first steps toward independence. Without fail, well-meaning people see a young fawn alone and conclude it is lost or abandoned and in danger. They put out a call to the warden to come and get it. So off we go.

Tending to a young fawn is a tedious and extremely difficult task. It's nearly impossible to meet the needs of the young critter as their mother would, even if we had the time. I responded many times to these calls, and I'd always wonder if the animal was indeed abandoned or if the mother was simply watching her baby take the steps she knew were essential for its survival.

One March, I responded to a call about a wounded deer lying along a road in Monroe. I found the homely little buck sprawled out in a ditch, desperately trying to lift its head so it could flee, but it was too malnourished to do so.

Adding to the poor little creature's homeliness was the gruesome sight of one foot that was severely swollen and deformed, probably the result of an old injury, possibly from a vehicle or hunting mishap.

The deer had obviously been through some rough times during the recent weeks of heavy snow and brutally cold weather, and my first thought was to unholster my revolver and put the poor thing out of its misery. But there was something about those piercing brown eyes that just wouldn't allow me to destroy it.

The little buck licked my hand while I gently stroked its head, trying to keep it calm. He showed no fear as I knelt alongside him, pondering what to do next. I replaced my firearm in its holster and reassured him I'd make every effort to rehabilitate him, hoping to give him a few more days here on earth. I gently picked him up and placed him on the back-seat of my cruiser for the short trip back to the Ford ranch.

Now I faced the battle of convincing Mrs. Ford that we had a new addition to the household, for better or worse. I'd lay on the old excuse of how it was my civic duty to shelter and care for my latest find. I knew that once she stared into those penetrating brown eyes she'd agree to give the critter another chance, especially now that the brutal cold winter was nearly over and he'd survived the worst of the season.

The young animal hardly moved during the slow drive to my house, but it kept staring at me with those big brown eyes.

As expected, Mrs. Ford was reluctant at first, but she agreed I could keep the deer in our cellar until it either won its fight to survive or succumbed to its injuries. By now, she was accustomed to having one creature or another roaming our household. She'd put up with owls flying freely between the rooms and a partridge perched precariously on the back of our couch. What harm could a cute little fawn do?

There was only one time when she defiantly refused to accept one of my guests. She returned home from work and

I greeted her with the news that we had a young blue heron perched in our bathtub.

"Just how to hell do you think I'm going to be able to take a bath?" she sputtered.

"Oh, just push him over, he'll move," I tried to reassure her. But it wasn't about to happen. She was quite adamant about not sharing the bathtub with any long-legged, pointed-beak flying creature.

I was ordered to take my damned heron elsewhere, regardless of its possible fate. She didn't like him, period. I got the impression from watching the heron that the feeling was mutual, but I didn't dare say so.

I carted the prehistoric-looking bird back to the lake, hoping Mother Nature might take care of it, but the next morning the bird was dead.

For the most part, though, Judy was receptive to the orphans and injured creatures of the wild and for that I was indeed thankful.

A few bales of loose hay, a bucket of fresh water, and a large gathering of fresh cedar branches, along with a bushel or two of apples donated by an orchard in nearby Winterport, were spread on my cellar floor.

The newly named Bucky found himself in an environment that offered some hope for his future. Within minutes, he was enthusiastically munching away on the load of goodies, a sure sign that perhaps he'd make it after all.

For the next few weeks I found myself constantly scraping up deer poop, changing hay, and carting in fresh cedar limbs and apples. I watched as Bucky replaced the weight he had lost, rebuilding his strength in the process.

In no time, Bucky was able to stand and walk on his own. Whenever I got near him, he'd wag his tail and run my

way. Occasionally, he'd gently butt me in the rear in a playful sort of way, indicating he wanted to have his head
scratched.

It took a few weeks, but Bucky was back to as normal as
I figured he could be. It was time to make arrangements to
reintroduce him to the wild where he belonged.

I searched for a secure place to release him, a place
where he wouldn't get shot or harmed by poachers or fall
victim to a predator in search of a little fresh meat. Bucky's
foot never improved. He still walked with an awkward limp,
but it didn't seem to hinder his ability to run and jump.

Eventually I arranged to release Bucky at Baxter State
Park in northern Maine. This would be the ideal spot for
him, alongside a ranger's camp. It would provide him with
some protection from hunters and the support he might
require to adjust back into the wild.

The long ride from Brooks to Baxter was quite interesting. Bucky stood on the backseat for most of the way, anxiously looking out the window as the scenery passed him by.

Along the way we were stopped by a flagman at a con-
struction site. We were the first in line. Casually, this traffic
guru glanced at my cruiser as the deer stood peeking out the
window, watching his every move.

It was obvious the image of a deer watching him didn't
really sink in as he looked back at the oncoming traffic
without so much as a blink of his eye. All of a sudden he
came to, whirled back around, and began shouting, "You've
got a gawd-damned deer in the back of your car!"

The dazed flagman acted as if I didn't have a clue that
Bucky was in the backseat. Rushing toward us, he kept
shouting, "There's a deer on your backseat!"

I felt like saying, "No shit, you roadside genius," along with a few other choice remarks, but instead I remained as professional as I could.

"I know," I calmly responded. "It's a deer I've rehabilitated. I'm taking him to a place where he can be released back into the wild."

Eventually, Bucky and I arrived at his new home at the ranger's camp at Baxter State Park. I opened the back door of the cruiser and he cautiously stepped out, then casually trotted over to the woods, sniffing the leaves and branches around him. He began to leap around in what appeared to be sheer joy and excitement for his return to freedom. It was a sight to behold.

Fortunately, Bucky had escaped the bullet to his head that I'd contemplated to end his misery a few weeks before. He'd been spared to live in a world that hopefully would appreciate his presence. Homely as he was, Bucky had a friendly personality that was second to none. Those piercing dark brown eyes would mesmerize even the hardest of villains. It was those eyes, along with his personality, that gave him a new lease on life, and I was proud of my part in his success.

As he slowly walked into the bushes, Bucky turned around one last time, intently staring in my direction. It was as if he was saying, "Thank you. Thank you, sir, for granting me another chance."

I quietly whispered, "You're welcome, deer," and got back into the cruiser and headed for home, wondering what kind of a critter would become my houseguest the next time around.

The Game Warden and the Murderer

For nearly thirty years I've had a respectful relationship with a notorious poacher-turned-murderer named Joel Fuller. Lately, Joel has opened up more than ever about a life in crime unrivaled in our rural county.

He resides in a federal prison in Pennsylvania and will never be released. That's what convictions for two drug-related murders have meant for him. Our paths crossed numerous times before he was incarcerated, always sending shivers of tension through me.

Once, he had a shotgun aimed at the head of a warden he believed was me as he was pursued in a dark field in the town of Morrill. That he didn't pull the trigger was a matter of luck: If the searching light had shone on him, a warden would have died, he's told me numerous times. Makes me shake my head just thinking about it.

Some have asked why I bother with Joel, whose contempt for society and the laws I was paid to uphold was extreme, to put it mildly. I'm not sure I can answer that, though I still look forward to our almost daily e-mails, through which I've gained insights into the way his mind works and how he carried out his crimes. But let's go back to the early 1980s, when Joel was an aggressive poacher who was called "The Deer Hunter" by his friends.

Joel was proud of that moniker. He thrived on hunting and fishing whenever and wherever he could. The fish and game laws were nothing more than a mild inconvenience as he followed his unsavory path.

In between his bouts of deer poaching, he committed several burglaries, thefts, and eventually a robbery that led to his involvement in murder-for-hire. It was a tragic downward spiral for the young man, who, from an early age, struggled with alcohol and drug abuse, along with a severely strained relationship with his father that caused him to live in fear at home.

Joel says his father repeatedly yelled at him, "You'll never amount to anything! I wish I could sell you, or get rid of you"—harsh words cast upon a young lad who was just starting out in life. Severe beatings went along with the barrage of hateful comments from the man he wanted to trust the most.

Joel resorted to running away from home and skipping school, eventually quitting altogether while abusing his body with a mixture of booze and drugs and embarking on a crime spree that was never-ending. He spent many hours alone, hanging out in the woods and living off the land.

As a law enforcement officer, I vaguely knew of Joel's family prior to the several criminal trials they watched their son endure. Not then aware of his father's abuse, I generally regarded his parents as decent folks who had their own world shattered by a child who had gone wildly astray. I could only imagine what they were going through, living in a small community where the family name had been smeared.

The incident with the shotgun occurred late one night in a field across from an adversary's home in Morrill. The farmer who owned the property accused Joel of constantly night-hunting in his field, even though Joel had given his word that he wouldn't hunt there.

That the farmer didn't believe Joel ticked him off, and Joel wanted revenge. His intent was to shoot a deer, cut out its heart, place it on a stake along with the shell casing from his illegal act, and set them up on the farmer's doorstep—in effect, saying to the farmer, accuse me if you will, but I'm not forgetting it.

After jacking a large buck, Joel dragged the carcass off into the woods. He quickly gutted it. He had concealed his crime well, making sure not to leave any traces.

Meanwhile, the farmer contacted the warden service to report gunshots in his field. A warden, whom Joel believed was me, arrived, and together the warden and the farmer made a cursory search looking for evidence of a night-hunting violation.

Joel, hiding behind a stone wall, awaiting a ride, watched the warden's light sweep aimlessly over the area.

"I'd made up my mind if the light lit me up, I was going to squeeze the trigger," he boasted to me later. "As your light was heading straight my way, I was putting pressure on the trigger, but fortunately for you, John Boy, that beam of light miraculously went right up over my head, and you walked right on by. You were so close, I could see the stripe of your uniform pants," he said. "You don't know how close you came that night."

I responded, "Joel, I can't believe you would shoot someone over a damned old dead deer."

"John Boy, in the frame of mind I was in at that time, there's no doubt in my mind I would've pulled the trigger. No doubt whatsoever," he insisted. "You really don't know how close you came to getting shot that night."

I've never told Joel that it wasn't me in that field.

On December 16, 1983, U.S. Navy officer Sonny Grotton was executed by an unknown assailant who waited behind a woodpile as Grotton walked toward his home in downtown Belfast, where his wife and children were waiting. Grotton was returning from Rhode Island, where he was stationed, to share Christmas with his family.

Joel became a prime suspect in the Grotton slaying. Rumors were running wild in Belfast that Grotton's wife had hired him to kill her husband. But without evidence to support a charge, it was several years before he was finally indicted.

About a year later, Joel murdered a noted cocaine dealer named Norman Grenier, who lived outside Belfast in the small town of Swanville. On that fateful day, Joel had met up with three of his criminal companions early in the afternoon. Together they had cruised through the area, looking to sell some stolen property they'd acquired. They all were drinking heavily along the way.

Joel knew that Grenier always had a large stash of cash at his home, the fruits of his lucrative but illegal business. Together, the four buddies decided that robbing Grenier would be a chance for some easy cash. Joel and his buddy Billy were dropped off at the end of the driveway leading up to Grenier's house. The other two men were instructed to come back in a half-hour to pick them up.

Unable to find an easy way into the house, Joel and Billy decided to bust through a large plate-glass window and surprise the unsuspecting residents. Grenier and his girl-friend were sitting on a couch directly beneath the window when the glass exploded all around them and Joel and Billy burst inside. Grenier reached for a gun.

Joel reacted instantaneously, shooting Grenier at point-blank range with his sawed-off shotgun. Grenier never knew what hit him; his girlfriend covered her head in a blanket, fearing that she would be next. Joel told Billy to make sure she didn't move while he ransacked the house for the large amount of cash that he never did find.

As quickly as they'd entered, they were back out of the house, waiting for their cronies to pick them up.

Thanks to an informant, it didn't take police long to fig-ure out who had killed the drug dealer, and Joel and his three cohorts were arrested. At his initial court hearing, Joel posted bail and was allowed to remain free pending his trial, which would be a few months down the road.

The Grenier murder caused a swift change of plans among several law enforcement agencies that had been plan-ning a sting operation to nab cocaine dealers in the area. Instead of the sting, anyone they thought might be helpful was brought in for questioning. Many of these suspects were quick to cooperate with the authorities, hoping to save their own skins in the process. Some of them openly wondered if they might be the next victim of a shotgun blast.

As the noose began to tighten, a local cocaine kingpin sought out Joel, knowing that he was capable of committing murder if the price was right. Joel had already been charged with one murder and had nothing to lose.

I'll call the kingpin Martin, which isn't his real name. Martin was desperate to hire someone to protect his own interests and to silence those who might try to implicate

him in the drug business. Joel was offered $10,000 for each
hit he'd make at Martin's direction. He was given the best
equipment to carry out his dastardly deeds—a variety of
rifles with top-notch scopes, surveillance and camouflage
gear, advance money, cars, and more.

Martin told Joel to secretly stalk seven men from
Augusta to Blue Hill who appeared to be cooperating with
the authorities. Joel was to know exactly where these men
were at any given time, and when Martin gave the order,
Joel was to kill them as soon as possible. Martin assured Joel
he'd be immediately paid for his services.

Joel took his job seriously, stalking the men, knowing
their every routine, where they lived, worked, and hung out,
and who their close acquaintances might be. On more than
one occasion, he actually hid and dry-fired on some of them
as they nonchalantly went about their business, unaware of
the danger lurking behind them.

One of the first individuals who decided to cooperate
with the authorities to save his own neck was a young man
from Northport by the name of Scott Lacombe. Although
Joel had been scouting several other men for days on end,
Martin had moved Lacombe to the top of his hit list.

The evening before Lacombe's scheduled appearance
before a federal grand jury in Bangor, Martin called Joel in a
panic, authorizing him to make the hit ASAP.

Joel calmly pulled into Lacombe's dooryard, where he
blew the horn, hoping that Lacombe would come outside.
Instead, Lacombe's fiancée walked out to see who was there.
She was on an all-time high, as Lacombe had asked her to
marry him earlier that afternoon.

Joel told the woman he was a friend of Lacombe's and
asked her to have him come outside to talk.

A few moments later, Scott wandered out into the drive-way where he received a double-barrel shotgun blast of buckshot to his head, killing him instantly. His terrified bride-to-be witnessed the murder from the kitchen window.

Having successfully completed his first mission, Joel raced out of the area, hiding the shotgun on a back road to be picked up later. He then went to a local bar where Martin was waiting. Joel casually strolled by Martin, sitting at the bar, signaling for him to go into the men's room where they'd have some privacy. "Scott is no longer available," Joel proudly informed his boss.

A gratified Martin handed Joel a large fistful of cash, promising to pay him the rest the next day. "Go home and stay out of sight for now," he told Joel. "I may want you to do some others right off quick. I'll be in touch."

Before Joel's murder spree could go any further, State Police were hot on his trail for the Lacombe homicide, having been provided a good description of the shooter by Lacombe's fiancée. Within hours he was taken to the Waldo County Jail, where he was placed in a lineup.

The girlfriend was brought in to make a positive identification of Joel, which would help prosecutors make their case against the deer hunter.

"I knew she was very nervous and extremely scared," Joel has reported to me. "And I knew that if I could stare right into her eyes, she wouldn't dare make a positive identification by picking me out of the group."

Apparently his scheme worked, because in the end she didn't pick him out of the lineup.

The investigating detectives disgustedly told Joel that the girlfriend was 97 percent sure it was him, but she couldn't be positive. That wasn't enough for them to hold him. Once again, Joel was allowed to go free, but this time the State Police were breathing down his neck on almost every move he made.

His car was impounded a few days later and taken to the crime lab in Augusta. The investigators dismantled it, looking for evidence tying him to the Lacombe homicide. Finding none, they were forced to give it back. Joel had to put the seats and dashboard together before he could leave the crime lab. The police watched him do so, but refused to help him.

A few days later, a contingent of officers confronted Joel with a warrant for his arrest. They were planning to bring him before a judge to revoke his bail in the Grenier case.

Joel, knowing he would be taken into custody, escaped into the thick woods—he wasn't about to go willingly.

Over the next several days, many of us in law enforcement spent countless hours canvassing the area and following up leads as we looked for Joel. We didn't know he was hiding out on an island in an area known as Witcher's Bog in Searsmont. He knew every inch of the bog, and from his perch high up in a tree he watched as the police searched.

With winter weather settling in, Joel traveled strictly at night and usually between snowstorms so as not to leave any tracks. He sought shelter in a camp a short distance from the bog, gaining access by climbing a tree and then carefully lowering himself down to a side window that he knew from previous experience had been left unlocked. Once safely inside, he turned on an electric heater and watched from the upstairs bedroom as the police occasionally checked the area. He slept upstairs with his loaded shotgun close by. He was determined to shoot anyone who approached. He stayed there for a few days before moving on.

Several days later, his sister convinced him to turn himself in before he or others were killed. She told him that
family members were being followed everywhere, and that
she really wasn't sure it was the police who were tailing
them. They were all scared.

Joel agreed to turn himself over to his attorney and to
State Police trooper Harry Bailey. They met at a pre-
arranged location where Joel was finally taken into custody.
He was immediately brought before a judge, who revoked
his bail and sent him to prison to await his trials, the first
being for the Grenier homicide. Joel was found guilty and
sentenced to fifty years in prison.

In June of 1990, I retired from the Warden Service and
was elected Waldo County sheriff a few months later. In
June of 1993, my third year as the county's chief law-
enforcement officer, it was my responsibility to provide
security in Superior Court during Joel's second murder trial,
for the death of Scott Lacombe. After eight long years, the
case would finally be heard before a jury of Joel's peers.

It was a hectic and stressful time, especially after we
were told of Joel's plans to escape during the trial. One of
his friends told me that Joel intended to have a handgun
smuggled into the courtroom to help him make a bold getaway. The courtroom escape called for him to take his attorney hostage with the gun held to his head, using him as a
human shield. He and a female cohort then planned to make
their escape to a campsite well off the beaten trail in
Searsmont that had been provisioned for their use.

After a meeting of several officials from my agency, the
State Police, the prison, and the Attorney General's office, a
plan was put in place, and the phone that Joel had use of at
the super-max prison was wiretapped. Then, word on the

street had it that Martin wanted Joel killed before he could testify against him, detailing his role in the murder-for-hire scheme.

Thus, every day of transporting Joel the thirty miles from the prison in Warren to court in Belfast was a distinct challenge that required additional troopers, deputies, prison officials, and officers from other agencies. Joel was handcuffed and placed in leg irons, ensuring he wouldn't escape on foot. He was secured to the backseat of the prison van by straps and escorted by fully armed State Police officers traveling in front of the prison van and behind. Officers would move ahead along the route and block off each intersection so the prison van could pass without slowing down. We were taking no chances.

On the very first day of the trial, while a jury was about to be selected, I walked Joel into the courthouse. I pointed out the deputies stationed around the entrances. They were armed with fully automatic weapons and had a clear view of the streets.

"Joel, I just want you to know right up front that should you walk or run out through those doors unescorted, you'll never make it across the street," I told him. "These guys have their orders, and let there be no doubt they'll carry them out."

I can still see his face as he looked at me, grinning from ear to ear. "I got your message, John. You won't have any problems on my end, I assure you," he said. And thankfully, we didn't.

Jury selection created yet another fiasco of sorts. When the court couldn't find enough unbiased citizens to form a panel, the judge called me into her chambers and handed me a fistful of blank subpoenas.

"I want you to go out on the street and find a group of Waldo County citizens. You give them a subpoena and tell them they have fifteen minutes to appear in court to serve as a potential juror," she demanded.

In addition, another list of prospective jurors from the outskirts of town was drawn from the jury-pool so that more subpoenas could be served on a host of residents.

Judge Margaret Kravchuck got her jury, but she made a lot of folks quite unhappy with my department.

The weeklong trial proceeded with a couple of incidents that raised the security level a bit, but in the end the testimony concluded, and the case was sent to the jury. Everyone thought it would be a quick verdict, but it wasn't.

The jury reached an impasse and had to be sequestered overnight at a local motel, where security was tight lest someone try to interfere with the process. Eventually, the jurors found Joel guilty of the crime as charged. A few days later, he was sentenced to a life term on top of the fifty-year sentence he already was serving. (Kingpin Martin, now deceased, was never identified and thus never charged, although Joel has identified him to me since.)

During the jury's deliberations, Joel and I talked about deer hunting and some of his other experiences over the years. Once again he talked of the dark night when he almost shot a warden in the farmer's field. He was still determined that warden was me.

A few months passed and one day I received a large oil painting created by The Deer Hunter himself, who had become a decent artist behind bars.

It depicted a wild-looking cowboy firmly holding a shotgun with both barrels pointed directly at the viewer. It was his not-so-subtle way of reminding me of how close I'd come to being his first murder victim.

In the Grotton case, Joel was found not guilty, although Grotton's wife was convicted of murder-for-hire.

Today, Joel admits he is right where he belongs. He has resigned himself to the fact that he will never again roam the countryside as he once did. With nothing to lose, he is open and occasionally humorous about his dark past.

In our many communications, he reminds me of a time when the violence we all assumed only occurred in faraway places actually reared its ugly head in my own neighborhoods. I have a strong, deep hope that it won't happen again.

Foot-jack-uh!

At the top of my "most wanted" list were the night-hunters, mostly because they knew exactly what they were doing. They obviously were trying to outwit their local warden, and we wardens were trying to be smart enough to rope them in. For the most part, the advantage was theirs.

By far the cagiest of the night-hunters were those who walked out to a remote spot near their homes with a hand-held light and a rifle. These "foot-jack-uhs," as I called them, usually dressed warmly for the occasion and were extremely familiar with the countryside they hunted.

Unlike those lazy nincompoops who hunted from a warm pickup with a plug-in spotlight, flashing one field after another, hoping to catch a big buck grazing in the black of night, these foot-jack-uhs were serious in their efforts.

I had a close call nabbing a foot-jack-uh early in my career in a remote section of Burnham. I barreled across the field running as fast as my fat little legs would carry me, gaining on my man.

It was one of those nights when it was darker than the inside of a rubber boot. It was also another one of those times when I'd failed to grab my flashlight. The next thing I knew, I went sailing headfirst into the puckerbrush as my legs snagged on a barbed-wire fence along the wood line.

Needless to say, my foot-jack-uh knew the area far better than I did. The last I heard of him, the brush was breaking far ahead of me as he scurried off into the dark of night and I lay stunned in the muck along the edge of the field.

Oh, well. You win a few and sometimes you lose in the competitive activity known as law enforcement. That night, I was on the losing end.

A short time later was a different story. It was a dark, frosty night as I parked on an old tote road adjacent to the Hemlock Hill Road in Unity. Nearby was a green field that looked enticing to anyone searching for a big buck feeding under the cover of darkness.

I'd just poured myself a cup of hot coffee and was settled inside the comfort of my cruiser, watching, waiting, and listening, wondering if this was the right spot to be.

A burst of light swept the field around me. At first I thought I might be seeing things because my eyes had a tendency to play tricks on me in the black of night.

I rolled down the window. Once again a beam of light swept the nearby field, only this time it appeared to be getting closer.

My heart started racing as I anticipated the mess I'd be facing in a few minutes. Without a doubt, I knew there'd be one—there always was—as it looked like I might catch up with a foot-jack-uh.

I got out of the cruiser, making sure I had my flashlight gripped tightly in my hand.

The wait was on as I scanned the darkness, hoping to see signs of movement. My ears were open, too, listening for any rustle of footsteps.

I heard a quiet shuffling. They'd walk a short distance and stop. There'd be nothing but dead silence before they'd continue walking again.

Each time, a burst of light lit up the field and the surrounding area. They obviously were searching for the yellow eyes of a whitetail.

Eventually, I made out the silhouettes of two men, traveling side by side. I assumed one of them had the gun while the other was operating the light. They were still a few yards away, coming directly toward me.

My heart was pounding wildly, and I actually feared they'd hear it long before they reached me. I remained completely still, waiting for the right moment to ambush them, hoping not to get shot in the process.

Crunch, crunch, crunch. Their feet crushed the frozen ground as they walked. Again they stopped, briefly lighting up the back of the field. I thought they'd never reach me.

Crunch, crunch, crunch. They were getting closer. I remained motionless, tucked up against a tree along the edge of the field. I could barely see them as they slowly inched my way.

It was show-and-tell time! I jumped out of the woods, aiming my light directly at them while at the same time screaming, "Game warden—hold it right there!"

You'd have thought I'd painted raw turpentine on their bare butts as they both screeched, which ended up scaring the hell out of me. It didn't slow them down one bit, though, as they shot out across that field like a couple of racehorses running the Kentucky Derby. They knew there was a lot at stake for both of them, and they needed to get away as soon as possible.

Wisely, they separated, leaving me with no choice but to pursue the one closest to me. He was a big one, too, easily six feet tall and built like a football linebacker. Considering his size, I was amazed at how fast he could run. We zigzagged across the field and eventually onto Hemlock Hill Road. I was gaining on him, which for me was a minor miracle.

Finally, I was close enough to make a lunge for him, grabbing him around the neck. Down we went, rolling around in the ditch like a couple of tired-out pigs in a pig scramble at a country fair.

I was completely out of breath and so was he. As I lay on top of him like a beached whale, pinning him to the ground, I told him he was under arrest.

Neither of us could've gone much farther, nor did we have the strength to fight or struggle.

Regaining my composure, I managed to handcuff him. I was gasping between breaths while attempting to read him his constitutional rights—the right to remain silent and blah-blah-blah.

He said his name was Rodney and that he was from Bridgewater, Massachusetts. His driver's license confirmed this information. Other than that, Rodney refused to say who was with him or answer any of the other questions I asked as we hiked back to the cruiser for the long, quiet ride to the Waldo County Jail.

"Rodney, I don't suppose you know a fellow by the name of Grover, do you?" I inquired.

I suspected there might be some connection between Rodney and Grover, the area's notorious poacher, seeing that some of Grover's relatives lived a short distance away and my past experiences revealed that many of Grover's hunting buddies came from the same Massachusetts area as Rodney.

"Grover! Grover who? I ain't never heard of any #$@%*& Grover!" he replied.

"I'm sure you probably haven't," I smartly responded. No sense doing any more talking, I thought.

I booked Rodney into the county facility, charging him with night-hunting, and requested that the jail notify me if anyone showed up to post his bail.

Amazingly, within a few hours of my departure, I received a radio message from the jail staff. "Warden Ford, your man was just freed on bail. A fellow by the name of Grover arrived with plenty of cash to finalize the deal."

Surprise, surprise! Without a doubt, either Grover or one of his nearby relatives more than likely had accompanied Rodney that night on Hemlock Hill, but proving it would be impossible.

Oh, well. Even though I hadn't successfully captured both of them, at least I'd finally bagged my first foot-jack-uh. I'd simply have to wait and see what Grover's demeanor might be the next time we met. I was sure he'd have something to say.

Night-Hunting for Drug Smugglers

Most of a game warden's work involves people we know doing the same stuff they've done for years. Occasionally, though, we get the call to assist in matters involving total strangers, like the members of the Florida-based Zion Coptic Church who set up a headquarters nearby as a front for a drug-smuggling operation.

The State Police suspected a huge shipment of baled marijuana—tons of it—was to be smuggled into the region from along the coast. The shipment was en route to Maine from the southern seas, but the exact date and time of arrival were not known.

My State Police buddy, Sergeant Harry Bailey, was in charge of the smuggling unit, and Warden Sergeant Bill Allen and I were assigned to monitor any comings and goings from a rural residence in the town of Stockton Springs.

The marijuana, once unloaded from the mother ship in nearby Stonington, was to be moved to the Stockton Springs property and eventually shipped across the country for distribution. It was an elaborate operation, to say the least.

Ironically, a few months earlier, this sect had purchased a number of buildings, including greenhouses, from Bill Allen's in-laws, so Bill was familiar with the location and layout of the property we'd be watching from afar.

Group members tried not to draw attention to themselves by paying for the entire Stockton Springs estate in cash—hardly a means of avoiding attention in a place where paying cash for a Happy Meal at McDonald's was a struggle for many.

As the expected arrival date neared, Bill and I sat in his cruiser on a rural country road surrounded by fields a short distance away from the estate. It was a perfect location. We could see anyone coming and going from the place, and at the same time we could work night-hunters around us. The fields were full of deer every night we were in the area.

In the backseat of the cruiser was Satan, Bill's trained K-9. Satan was great for tracking folks who tried to escape and for recovering evidence tossed during a crime.

Later that evening, a car slowly cruised past us on the narrow country road. Within seconds, we were startled by two loud shots. Bill pulled down to the edge of the road, just in time for us to see the car drive around the bend at the foot of the hill heading away from us.

There was no doubt these folks had just shot at something in the field below us, more than likely a deer.

I got out of the cruiser and ran down along the roadside, listening and watching to see if someone had been dropped off to retrieve whatever they'd shot. It was extremely dark and quiet as I worked my way down over the hill, watching for any activity in the large field.

Bill remained in the cruiser with Satan. If I saw someone, I was to signal Bill with my flashlight, and he'd scoot on down with the dog.

I could hear two men talking as they headed my way on foot. "I'm sure I hit it. It looked like a nice buck," I heard one say to his buddy.

I ducked behind a large pine tree across the road from the field, waiting to see what these men were up to. Hopefully, we'd catch them retrieving the fruits of their crime.

Within minutes, they were less than twenty feet from me. They wandered into the field searching for the deer. I patiently waited to catch them with the goods. After all, it would be much easier to have them drag the deer back to the road than doing it myself.

To my surprise, the two men started running back my way with a wounded buck hobbling along in front of them. The deer was coming straight toward me with the men close to its tail. My heart pounded as I wondered what the next few minutes would bring. I only hoped they didn't have a rifle with them, as I was directly in the line of fire.

I sucked in behind that pine tree like a wart on a toad's rump, listening to the thumping of footsteps heading my way. First came the beat of animal hooves running across the tarred road in front of me. The buck passed within three feet of my hiding place, crashing through the bushes as it made its escape.

Close behind the wounded deer was the dim beam of a flashlight bobbing up and down, also heading toward me. It was show-and-tell time.

As one of the men scampered onto the paved road, I jumped out from behind the pine tree and aimed the bright beam of my flashlight directly in his eyes. "Game warden! Hold it right there, gentlemen!" I yelled.

The man, armed with a dim flashlight and a large hunting knife, stood paralyzed, screaming so loudly it scared the hell out of me. His little legs were jumping up and down, but he wasn't going anywhere. It was a sight to behold.

"It's the #$@%*& wardens!" he yelled to his partner, who was still out in the field trying to catch up.

I arrested him for night-hunting, while signaling for Bill with my flashlight that it was time for Satan to do a little tracking for the other culprit who'd fled back into the tall grass.

There was no question I'd scared the living bejeezus out of my poor arrestee as he stood frozen in the road. I tried to calm down his fragile nerves while reading him his Miranda rights. Miranda rights are those legalities that are required to protect folks like him from mean old cops like me. God forbid he should be allowed to confess his sins freely.

As Bill turned Satan loose into the tall grass, he shouted, "You might as well give it up—there's a K-9 heading your way!"

Within seconds, a head popped up out of the tall grass like a woodchuck peeking out of its den. The man began screaming, "Don't turn him loose! I give up, I give up!"

He scampered our way to receive his own private reading of the Miranda rights.

Once everyone had somewhat calmed down, the first night-hunter inquired, "How to hell did you guys get here so quickly?" Of course, we couldn't tell him our reasons for being around there in the first place.

Most of us Maine folks had no idea what was occurring along our coastline and in our own backyards, and neither did I until my pal Harry Bailey brought me into the fold on this latest adventure.

The Maine coast was considered to be the number-one port of entry for illegally imported marijuana from the southern seas. The Stonington escapade was just one such event that occurred that year, and what an event it was.

The ship into Stonington eventually arrived a few nights later, loaded with more than sixty tons of baled marijuana and felons who scattered themselves throughout the countryside, just like our two night-hunters. And just like them, they paid for their illegal activities, big-time.

Right on Time

We were in the third night of being parked in the same old spot on the lookout for reported night-hunters. All was quiet, just the baying of coyotes and the hoots of a nearby owl to break the silence.

At about two in the morning headlights were slowly coming our way. I'd been half asleep, snuggled comfortably behind my cruiser's steering wheel. My partner, Norman Gilbert, was purring away like a little Partner chain saw stuck in high gear.

"Wake up, Norman! Wake to hell up! We've got company coming," I yelled, as the headlights entered the clearing below us.

Norman sprang to life just as the truck came to a sudden stop. Two loud rifle shots followed.

Within a minute or so, the truck came our way. As it passed us, I pulled in behind it without using my lights. Once we were neatly tucked in behind the back bumper so we could witness any evidence that might be tossed out the windows, I signaled for them to stop.

The three Massachusetts hunters pulled over. Inside their truck was a large handheld spotlight, a loaded rifle, and two empty shell casings rolling on the floor. We arrested them for night-hunting and hauled them off to the local Crowbar Hotel to post bail for a future court appearance.

Under questioning, these half-inebriated nonresidents admitted they had fired their weapon, but only at a tree alongside the road.

It was kind of hard to accept the notion that these men had traveled all the way to the state of Maine, to a desolate back road at two in the morning, solely for the purpose of shooting a tree. Surely they could have come up with a better excuse than that—but then again, I suppose they had to say something.

Exercising their legal rights, these folks hired a local attorney to represent them at a jury trial held at Skowhegan Superior Court.

The main bone of contention was the amount of time that passed from when the shots were fired until their truck reached the spot where Norman and I were parked. Their attorney was attempting to raise the issue that it was possible someone else had fired the shots.

Norman's report said it was exactly one minute from the time the shots were fired until the truck reached us. I had already testified that, in my opinion, it was, indeed, approximately a minute between the two events.

The defense attorney grilled me hard, insinuating that maybe it was more than a minute. I held my ground without fully committing to an exact time frame.

Then it was Norman's turn to testify. He had been barred from the courtroom during my testimony so he hadn't heard what I'd said or the attorney's line of questions.

"Warden Gilbert, would you kindly tell this court and the jury just how long it was from the moment you heard the rifle shots until my clients reached your location? I wish to remind you, Warden Gilbert, I hope you'll do so according to the same facts you have here in your written report," the young attorney pleaded, waving the report in front of Norman's face.

"Yes sir, it was exactly one minute," Norman responded.

I could see the attorney's eyes brighten.

"Are you sure it was exactly a minute and no longer?" he repeated.

"Absolutely. No question about it," Norman said.

I knew what was about to happen. I was petrified as to how sure Norman was in his response, knowing damn well that Norman couldn't tell an exact minute from ten. I worked with the old boy, and I knew he didn't have a clue.

The young attorney bristled up to the witness stand. "Okay, Warden Gilbert, let me get this straight. You claim it was exactly one minute before my clients reached your location. Is that correct, sir?"

"Yes, sir, as I stated, exactly a minute, and that's what it was. No more, no less."

Seizing the opportunity, the defense attorney said, "I want to conduct a little experiment here, Warden Gilbert. I'm going to time you, and I want you to tell this jury exactly when a minute is up. No more, no less. Would you be willing to do that, Warden?"

"I'll be glad to," Norman sputtered.

I thought to myself, Oh, God, there goes our case out the window. Surely Norman won't be within a hill of beans of even coming close to being accurate.

I monitored my watch, as did everyone else present. A dead and eerie silence encompassed the entire courtroom.

The seconds were slowly ticking by. At one point I looked up and Norman was smiling as he glanced about, calm as a cucumber. At exactly one minute Norman calmly said, "I believe that's a minute, sir!"

It was exactly one minute, without a second to spare.

I couldn't believe it. The old buzzard was precisely on the mark and in doing so he had taken the wind out of the defense attorney's sails.

Norman had obviously impressed the twelve jurors as to his credibility; they were smiling from ear to ear at him and his wisdom.

With his main argument shot all to hell, the defense attorney quickly rested his case. His little experiment had failed him miserably.

The deliberations took only fifteen minutes before the three nonresidents were all found guilty of the offense as charged.

As we were leaving I inquired of Norman, "How to hell did you pull off that little courtroom stunt? You were right exactly on the mark and without a second to spare."

"Nothing to it," the old goat chuckled. "That gawd-damned attorney didn't have a clue. I nonchalantly kept glancing up at the wall clock in the back of the courtroom, watching the second hand as it made its sweep around the board. I knew I couldn't miss!

"He was a real dumb-ass, don'tcha, think?" Norman grinned.

Don't Mess with Blinky

The use of decoy deer to catch night-hunters became acceptable to the warden department—and the courts—in the early 1980s.

The practice was controversial to some folks who felt it was a form of entrapment. Defense attorneys screamed loud and long about the unfairness of the decoys. For the most part, though, the use of a decoy as evidence was upheld in court.

The argument in favor of placing a silhouette deer in a field or along the edge of a clearing after dark was that it provided a night-hunter with exactly what he was searching for. The presence of a decoy didn't force a hunter into flashing a light on it or, in many cases, shooting at it. We had to assume that the spotlight, or the shot, represented a clear intention to night-hunt.

The department, of course, wouldn't pay for the facsimiles, but many of us wardens fashioned our own with Augusta's blessing. I called my mine "Blinky," and it originated in a freak sort of way. It was created by a retired law enforcement officer and an old friend of mine, former Waldo County chief deputy Leroy "Roy" Thomas of Morrill.

Roy, an ingenious sort, devised a set of electronic eyes that were operated remotely by batteries and a radio-control box, which were the only remnants of a model airplane kit I'd purchased earlier.

Not to change the subject, but my goal at that time was to find a new hobby. I'd made a substantial investment in building a radio-controlled airplane, hoping to learn how to fly it as skillfully as other folks were doing at the time. Roy was one of the best to learn from, and he was excited to have a new partner joining him at the homemade airstrip on his back lawn.

He assisted me every step of the way, especially when it came to hooking up the radio servers and attaching the engine to the plane. I'd spent the better part of a winter building it from scratch, stick by stick, detail by detail, following a thorough blueprint and set of instructions.

I was some proud of my finished product. It was elaborately decorated and pinstriped—a real classic, almost as if it was a real airplane.

Roy cleverly hooked his control box onto mine for the inaugural flight, just in case my inexperience might cause it to crash. That way, he could quickly assume the controls and safely land my masterpiece, rather than having it terminally crash and burn somewhere far away in his back fields.

In theory this so-called umbilical cord was a good plan, especially since I was a novice and he was a skilled pro at model airplane flying.

I remember sending the plane across the little airstrip and proudly launching it up into the heavens. As my confidence grew, I flew the little craft farther and farther away from Roy's house.

Roy was proud of my early success, just like a dad watching his kid perform some miracle feat, knowing that he'd played a vital role in the effort.

We were having the time of our lives, but now it was time to bring the craft back home before it ran out of gas.

As I banked the plane, I said, "I think you'd better land it, Roy. I don't know if I can bring it back down without staving it all to hell! I'll watch you the first time around."

Roy assumed the controls, and we watched the plane coming our way. Suddenly, it began wobbling, diving up and down, and then it went completely out of control.

"Are you doing that?" he anxiously inquired.

"Nope, I'm not touching anything," I assured him, as the plane went into a steep nosedive, disappearing behind his barn. There was a sickening thud and then nothing but dead silence.

We stood there staring at each other, then ran around to the back of the barn where we found a few pieces of balsa wood buried deep in the tall grass. There wasn't enough left of my plane to start a small fire.

So much for the dreams of pursuing a new hobby or any hopes of ever becoming a ground-based pilot.

We determined that the batteries operating the control unit had not been fully charged; thus, they went dead on our approach to Roy's airport, sending my masterpiece into the tailspin that brought about its demise.

As I picked up what was left of my hefty investment, I casually mentioned to Roy my plan to create a decoy deer in hopes of catching a night-hunter.

Roy was one of the smartest people I'd ever met when it came to inventing things. I could see that look on his face and a twinkle in his eyes, indicating that he was highly interested in assisting in the challenge.

A few days later Roy called to ask me to come to his house after dark. He had something special he wanted to show me.

My trusty companion, Deputy Game Warden Scott Sienkiewicz, and I arrived at Roy's home in the shadows of darkness. "Take a ride down the road and watch the field just before you get to the woods," he said, chuckling.

We jumped back into the truck and slowly cruised the road. Suddenly, from the ditch not very far away, a pair of eyes shined out. I was ready to hit the brakes, prepared to have a deer jump out in front of us.

I stopped alongside the highway where the eyes had been, only to be spooked by the blast of a siren.

Roy had invented a set of deer eyes using two small lightbulbs operated by the radio controls from my now-defunct airplane. They were attached to a metal rod stuck in the ground and surrounded by tall grass. He could turn them on and off by the mere flip of a switch, all the way from his house a good distance away.

Not only did this contraption give the appearance of a deer in the headlights, but Roy had also cleverly attached a small siren that he could turn on with another server, alerting those gawking at the woods that the cops were lurking nearby.

Thus it came to be that "Blinky, the miracle buck," was born. The electronic device was a sheer masterpiece as far as I was concerned.

Scott and I went back to Roy's, where he told us about scaring the bejeezus out of several people who had stopped at the same spot, thinking they were going to see a deer.

"You should have heard their tires squeal and watched them shoot to hell away from the area when I turned that siren on," he said, snickering deviously as I'd seen my old friend do so many times before.

Blinky was ready to be introduced to the poaching public. I couldn't wait.

Over time, Scott and I transformed Blinky into a life-size, painted plywood deer-silhouette, equipped with a large rack of antlers and glass eyes. We hooked the deer up to another server, using a rat trap and a door-spring to knock it down if someone shot at it. We'd spring the rat trap, which would release a pin holding the critter upright, causing it to fall over, thus giving the shooter the impression they'd bagged their quarry.

Some folks will do the damnedest things to bag a deer underneath the stars at night. But with Blinky watching, their joy was short-lived.

Leo and the Life Preservers

I'm not sure why, but I'd much rather shiver on the edge of a field on a frigid November night waiting for night-hunters than putt-putt around a lake on a beautiful summer afternoon trying to nab a fisherman for not having a license or life preservers.

The night-hunter is well aware that what he's doing is illegal, and he knows the consequences if he's caught. The unequipped fisherman likely was only careless and would make his situation right immediately if given the chance.

My aversion to lake patrol wasn't helped by the little puddle-jumping boat I was forced to use. It was a joke, and more than once, I'd signal for a boater to pull over only to have him smile as he sped away, ignoring my demands.

But my boss insisted that I trailer the little boat to Unity Pond and check fishermen as if they were major wrongdoers. It was good public relations, he told me. His parting words were, "I'll bet those folks don't even know they've got a game warden in the region."

With my little toy boat in tow, I shot down to the landing, swearing and sputtering all the way. I decided that every boat I checked that day wanted to be damn sure it was legal. I wasn't about to cut anyone an ounce of slack, no matter what his or her excuse might be. No exceptions!

The first boat I saw was occupied by an elderly gentleman. He was trolling a fishing lure behind the aluminum boat, hoping to catch a bass lurking along the shore.

"Morning, sir. How are they biting?" I inquired. Like I really cared.

"Nothing yet," he answered, smiling, as I pulled up alongside.

"Well, I'll be damned—you're a game warden?" He smirked. "I ain't never seen a warden out here before. Are you new to the area?"

For him to even ask such a silly question added more salt to an already-open wound. I wondered if perhaps this old geezer wasn't somehow in cahoots with my boss, recalling his very similar words.

"I've been around here for a while," I responded with a touch of sarcasm.

"Hmm," he said. "Just ain't never seen a warden on the pond before."

You just go right ahead and keep rubbing it in, you old geezer, I mumbled to myself.

I asked for his fishing license and boat registration, and couldn't help noticing that there were no life preservers in the open-bottom boat.

Aha! My first victim. The boss wanted production, and by the jeez, he was going to get it. I checked the registration and license to see if they were in order. The geezer's name was Leo.

Leo was rattling on about coming here from Arlington, Massachusetts, saying he was a longtime resident on the pond, living at a camp up at the farther end. He closed his little life statement with, again, "I still can't get over the fact I've never seen a warden on the lake before. Are you sure you ain't new?"

I didn't answer, but thought to myself, Leo, old buddy, when I get through with you in a few minutes, you won't want to see me out here again for a while.

"Leo, I noticed you don't have any life preservers in your boat. You know you're required to have them, don't you?"

His face turned a bright red as he feverishly looked around the boat.

"I had them right here; where'd they go?" he stuttered. "Damn it, damn it, I've left them back at the camp on the dock. I was in such a rush to get out here today I forgot 'em! Damn it all."

"Leo, I don't have any choice. I've got to give you a summons to court for failing to have your life preservers. It's the law, you know, and I just can't overlook it."

"Gee whiz, Warden, I know I left them on my dock. Can't you please follow me back there and I'll show you?"

"Sorry, Leo, the law's the law. No can do," I said, as I started making out the citation.

Personally, I felt terrible for what I was doing, but I was told to write tickets and to hold people accountable, so tickets and accountability it would be.

Poor Leo kept begging for me to please show a little compassion. "I never come out here without them," he pleaded.

"Sorry, Leo, but I have to treat everyone the same. I really don't have a choice," I said, as I continued writing out the ticket.

Leo then humbly inquired, "Warden, can I ask you something without sounding too offensive or wise to you?"

"What's that, Leo?" I inquired, without looking up from my writing.

"Well, Warden, I was just looking in your boat and I noticed that you don't have any life preservers either. Does that mean you guys are exempt from the rule?"

I felt the hairs standing up on the back of my neck as I slowly lifted my head and scanned the bottom of my boat for the preservers I hoped were there. They weren't. In my haste to make everyone as miserable as I was, I'd left my preservers stuffed in the trunk of my cruiser.

I looked over at Leo. "Leo, guess what?"

"What?" he inquired.

"Leo, you seem like a real nice fellow, and you know what? I think I'm going to cut you some slack today. Why don't you take your boat and go back and pick up your life preservers, and I'll go back and get mine. We'll forget we ever met out here today. How's that?"

"Oh, that sounds awful good to me, Warden, awful good. I promise you, I'll never forget them again."

"Well, Leo, it's a good lesson for the both of us, isn't it? You have a good day."

I restarted the motor and shot back toward my cruiser as fast as I could go, which wasn't very fast.

Once I got to the boat landing, I loaded the boat onto the trailer and headed for home. It was the shortest trip out on the lake I'd ever taken.

It Helps to Be a Damned Sneak

An informant who planned on trapping off an old tote road on the back side of a mountain in Monroe told me he found a set of illegal traps in the area, so I headed out.

I found two of the traps within a few yards of each other, just off the road, far away from any form of civilization. It was obvious they'd been there for a while, though it appeared they were being tended with some regularity, as there were ATV tracks in the dirt along the trail.

The traps lacked the proper identification, a violation in itself. The season was due to open the next day, so they were out of season as well.

I sprung the traps so I could tell if anyone came during the night to reset them. Then I made several deep impressions in the carefully sifted dirt, giving the appearance that some type of wild animal managed to escape the wrath of the metal jaws.

With my own trap now set, I snuggled in among the fir trees. I leaned up against the base of a tree that made a great backrest and commenced to read the book I'd brought along to bide the time.

Other than a partridge scaling through the alders in front of me and a small doe sneaking along the edge of the tote road, the afternoon wait concluded at darkness. I hiked back to my cruiser, deciding to return the next day.

Early that morning, I wandered back through the woods and into my den, ready for yet another day of waiting and watching. With my book in hand, I began passing the time, hour by hour, minute by minute. Patience was a definite requirement for this job, and I had plenty of it. Hell, why wouldn't I? Who else could take a book, hike into the woods, lean up against a tree, and spend an enjoyable day watching the wildlife around them while getting paid to do so? What a great job I had!

Like the day before, a couple of partridges winged past my location. A red squirrel occasionally taunted and chatted at me from a short distance away, irritated that I was treading on his sacred territory. But as before, no one came near the traps. I wondered if they knew I was around, even though to the best of my knowledge, no one had seen me coming or going.

At the edge of darkness, I again clambered out from underneath my blind. I planned on adding another charge for these culprits, if and when I ever made contact. By law, traps were required to be checked every twenty-four hours. I had carefully marked the location, and it was evident that no one had been there over that span.

The next day I'd bring more reading material. I had finished my book halfway through the day and got so bored that I passed the afternoon whittling away on a piece of wood with my pocketknife.

I arrived early armed with magazines, snacks, drinks—the works—ready to make another go of it. The sun slowly climbed above the trees from the east, bringing yet another

warm October day. I was immersed in my book when I
heard the putter-putter of engines coming my way.

My heart began to race. Could these be the culprits I'd
been waiting for?

Sure enough, the noise grew louder and louder, and
soon, two ATVs churned their way up the old tote road,
heading toward me.

The first stopped directly in front of the trap nearest to
me as the other machine continued on toward the second
trap. Both young gentlemen climbed from their rigs and
walked toward their illegal sets.

It was show-and-tell time. I slithered from underneath
my perch, quietly walking toward the burly lad standing
back-to, looking down on the sprung trap. He never heard
me coming as I shuffled in behind him.

"What the hell kind of animal is this?" he muttered,
hunched over, studying the strange prints I'd left behind in
the soft dirt.

Loudly and boisterously I said, "*I* was that kind of animal!"

A shotgun blast between his eyes wouldn't have shocked
this poor fellow any more than I had. He let out a screech
that could've been heard in downtown Bangor and scared
the living bejeezus out of me.

I asked him to pull up the trap and meet me by his ATV,
and I hustled up the trail to where his buddy had headed.
Apparently the buddy had overheard our conversation, as he
was desperately attempting to suck his large body behind a
small tree, hoping I wouldn't see him. I could see his shoul-
ders and one leg protruding from behind, so I ordered him
to come the hell out of there and to bring the trap with him.

I was familiar with both of these young men and was surprised to find them involved in such an activity. But then again, in this game, not much surprised me anymore. Even those I thought I knew quite well occasionally stepped over the line and violated a rule or two if they thought they could get away with it.

So my patience paid off. I wrote several summonses to hold them accountable for their sins and moved on. In the end, hopefully, these young fellows would learn to respect fish and game rules. They never knew when the beady eyes of a woods cop might be lurking nearby.

A few days later, I was told that I was being compared to a damned ghost who suddenly appeared out of nowhere in places where most men would never venture. It was a pleasant and complimentary comment, but in reality, like my fellow wardens, I was only doing my job.

Being a damned sneak happens to be one of the tools of the trade. If this was to be my reputation, I would accept it with grace.

A Ride-Along with the Boss

If ever there was a demoralizing experience for an employee of the Fish and Game Department, it was receiving those damned annual evaluation reports.

Our immediate supervisors filled out those reports to rate us on our overall job performance. They were intended to show the front office whether the employee was performing his duties to the level of perfection that a supervisor expected.

In other words, it was a judgment call by the boss, intended to either boost the morale of the employee by blowing a little smoke his way, or point out areas of concern where the employee needed to improve. Usually the evaluations did very little to improve relations.

Granted, none of us enjoys being criticized for doing our jobs in a manner most of us consider to be superb. However, there were times when a report showed we obviously had a few faults.

One of my biggest issues involved the care of my department-issued equipment, which I admit was not top-notch by any means. For example, I completely understood the extremely poor evaluation I received one year from a supervisor regarding my care of the boat stored behind the warden's camp in Burnham.

I was busy working day and night trying to capture every poacher in my district and completely forgot about the boat in my backyard, with its drain plug securely in place. The fall rains collected inside the fourteen-foot craft, filling it up to the seats with water that had no means of draining out.

When cold weather arrived, the water turned into a fourteen-foot block of solid ice. It wasn't until the boss showed up at the camp later that fall that he noticed my frozen bathtub. Needless to say, I wouldn't dare put into print the conversation he and I shared that day.

There were times, however, when I felt the boss was being a bit too picky. In those instances I found myself arguing the point, usually to no avail.

Once again the evaluation season arrived and Sergeant Bill Allen and I had our usual demoralizing confrontation. This one, however, was worse than any of the others I had experienced.

We met on Main Street in Brooks where, in his cruiser, I received the dreaded report card and reviewed it step by step. I was bluntly told that I was slack in my knowledge of what was going on in my district, along with a few other matters, even though I had worked a tremendous amount of hours with a schedule that most people would have considered intolerable.

I asked how he possibly could have come to such a conclusion.

"Well, for one thing, John, you don't check your bear-tagging stations as frequently as you should," he said—rather imperiously, I thought.

Immediately, I felt my blood pressure rising. I blurted out, "For cripe's sake, Bill, I've only had one bear tagged within my district in the past six years. Good Lord, if an agent had tagged one, he'd be so damned excited about it, I'd get a quick call from him."

Bear in my district were about as rare as canaries at the North Pole. But once again the boss made it clear he thought I should be stopping by the tagging stations, regardless.

There was going to be no compromise or persuasion that night. The tone was set, and it went downhill fast from there.

The next area we covered concerned my inability to get along with fellow officers and other agencies. I was completely baffled by this, seeing as I had recently been recognized as an honorary trooper by the Maine State Police for my efforts in working with them.

I reminded Bill how some members of my department had chastised me for spending what they considered was far too much time with the police.

"Yeah, but, John, you seem to spend most of your time in your own district, and not enough time working with other wardens," he went on.

Tempers were getting a little heated. It finally came to a head when I sarcastically accused him of having someone else make out the report. By then I'd pushed poor Bill over the edge. The next thing I knew, he was ripping the evaluation to shreds in a rage. Paper flew everywhere. I subtly reminded him it was against the law to litter, which didn't help my cause in the least.

We parted company that evening with our tires screeching, heading in opposite directions, madder than two men at war against each other.

Still, I realized that some of what the boss had mentioned were issues I needed to work on. It all boiled down to a difference in personalities and, like so many times before, this too would pass. Our personal friendship was too valuable for it to do otherwise.

The next time we met it was as cordial, friendly, and professional as before. We found ourselves chuckling about

Courtesy of John Ford Sr.

Warden John Ford and Sergeant Bill Allen found these illegal deer hanging from a tree in South China.

the uselessness of these damned efficiency reports as we
continued doing our jobs.

Later that fall, Lieutenant John Marsh unexpectedly
joined me for a night of working hunters in my district. We
were getting ready to head to a remote field in Burnham,
hoping to apprehend a violator or two, when I received a
radio call from Bill, requesting I start heading his way
toward Monroe. He was out by himself and it appeared
there was some night-hunting going on around him. Bill had
no clue the lieutenant was with me. The lieutenant grabbed
the radio and demanded that Bill meet him at a popular
truck stop in Hampden, quite some distance away, as soon
as possible.

I said, "What the hell are you doing, John?" He had a
devilish smirk on his face. I realized he was playing yet
another one of his practical jokes.

"I want to piss him off," he snickered.

Bill called me again, with disgust in his voice. "Did you
hear that radio traffic?" he sputtered. "I'll wait until you get
here so I can show you where to park. I think you're going
to have some business. Just as soon as I can get away from
the goddamned lieutenant, I'll come back."

John smiled, recognizing that part of his game plan had
already been accomplished. He jumped into the backseat of
my cruiser, instructing me to act as though I was alone.

We met up with Bill a short distance from where he'd
been parked. "Follow me," he said. "I'll show you where to
go. I have to meet with that gawd-damned lieutenant to see
what the hell he wants." He wasn't pleased.

I didn't dare let on that the "gawd-damned lieutenant"
was crouched on the floorboards of my cruiser, listening to
Bill spout off. How could I?

I headed down the narrow dirt road, going fast, following closely behind Bill. I purposely hit every bump I could, even recklessly swaying the car back and forth, listening to the lieutenant grunting and groaning as his head kept sliding into the side of the car.

"Where in hell are you headed?" he grumbled.

Soon I was parked in the spot where Bill had been. He sped off, headed for his meeting in Hampden, some fifteen miles away.

After a period of time had passed, I inquired, "How far are you going to let him get?"

"Oh, hell, he's got a ways to go." John snickered.

Finally, John radioed Bill to disregard. Without a doubt, I knew Bill would be fit to be tied.

"Convince him to get into your car when he gets back here," John said, smiling. "And don't let him know I'm here."

I was beginning to enjoy this myself, as I knew Bill was a jumper. The next few minutes could be quite interesting.

Eventually Bill returned. I asked him to join me in my cruiser and he did, launching into a verbal tirade, the likes of which I never expected.

"That gawd-damned, fat son of a #$@%*&! He could #$@%*& a dream!" he screamed.

I sank down in the seat, wondering what would transpire next.

John slowly rose up off the floor of my cruiser, quite proud of his accomplishments.

Immediately I ducked, as Bill's fists and arms began flying wildly all around the front of the cruiser. I was afraid he was going to break my windshield; flailing away, he looked like a heron trying to fly in a hurricane. He was trying to speak, but was so startled he couldn't.

Once he realized it was the lieutenant in the cruiser with us, he looked over at me in disgust, as if I'd initiated the entire prank. "You think your last efficiency was bad—you just wait until next year, you #$@%*&!"

"Hey, Bill, if you think mine's going to be bad, just what the hell do you think yours is going to be?" I chuckled. After all, the lieutenant was his supervisor and would be writing his evaluation. After that blast of profanities directed at his boss, I didn't think my evaluation would be the one to pay the price.

Every Town Has Its Cast of Characters

Without fail, every town in my patrol area had its share of memorable characters. You know—those types of folks who for one strange reason or another manage to stand out from the rest.

Many of the characters with whom I became so well acquainted had an attitude of total defiance for most of the laws governing our society—and they were oblivious to the consequences of their actions until they were caught red-handed. For the most part, I found these characters to be highly likable folks.

Grover, the so-called "Modern-day Robin Hood" and a skilled poacher, was one of these characters. He was intimidating to many, mainly because of his large size and deep raspy voice. He had a tendency to talk down in a rather authoritative manner to those he was addressing.

Folks credited Grover with shooting a hundred deer or more per year, most of them under the cover of darkness. Just listening to these stories made me wonder if the man ever got to sleep at all. But then again, my situation wasn't much better, as I tried night after night to catch him and others just like him in the act of committing their dastardly deeds.

It took a while for us to meet face-to-face. I'd been warned not to turn my back in his presence. But I sized him up as being amicable to a certain degree. The truth be known, after that first meeting with Grover, I respected and liked the man. We just happened to be on opposite sides of the fence regarding the fish and wildlife rules, that's all.

The Robin Hood title—one he thoroughly enjoyed— referred to his so-called philosophy that many folks who were up against hard times benefited from his illegal activities, as he supplied them with food for their table.

Our paths officially crossed several times. Some of our exchanges were quite pleasant, often with a bit of taunting each other in a friendly way. We had a few knock-down, drag-outs, too, involving just words; our tempers never flared to the point of becoming physical. One time we beat on each other's vehicles and held up traffic during a heated tirade in the middle of the highway, but that was the closest it came to going over the edge. A member of his party did end up getting a trip to jail as an indirect result of that incident, though.

We shared a mutual sense of respect that at times was almost comical to those who knew us both. In Grover's words, "I like you ten months out of the year. It's the other two months when I'd just as soon not have you anywhere around," referring to the busy hunting season.

Without fail, once the hunting season was over, I'd see Grover pulling into my dooryard. He expected a cup of coffee and an hour or more of ragging on each other over how the year had gone.

He would cheer about what he had gotten away with under my nose, and I'd remind him that I'd scheduled court hearings either for him or some of his cronies. I looked forward to the after-season coffee gathering.

Big Jim, from the town of Troy, was another character.

Jim was unusual just because of his size. He stood six feet, two inches tall and tipped the scales at well over 500 pounds. His unkempt beard and large round face made him appear even more of a giant.

I joked with him one day about the possibility of chasing him out through a field some night after he had blistered a big buck.

"Hell, John, I could eat a big box of ex-lax during the day to be fully ready just in case you decided to chase me at night," he chuckled.

Jim was jovial, slow-moving, manipulative, and sly as a fox. These are just a few of the words I'd use to describe him.

I first met Jim and Alan, his sidekick, working in the woods around Unity Plantation. Alan was doing the hard work while Jim maneuvered a skidder to and from the yard, a rather plush job compared to what Alan was tackling. Jim filled the entire cage of the mechanical monster, making it look like a toy.

Jim and Alan made a good pair—wherever you found one, you'd find the other. What one couldn't think of, the other could.

I vividly recall an occasion when I hauled Jim to court for a series of violations. The judge found him guilty of the charges and assessed a hefty fine. He also granted him a period of time to pay it off, with a stern warning that he would be arrested if he did not settle his debt on schedule.

As usual, Jim neglected to fulfill his obligations to His Honor. The judge angrily issued an arrest warrant, demanding I seize the giant and bring him immediately to the Waldo County Crowbar Hotel.

I spent the next few days searching for my buddy. It was obvious he knew I was in hot pursuit and had done whatever he could to avoid the inevitable. Several times I stopped by his house, knowing full well he was inside, but he wouldn't make his presence known. It was a challenging cat-and-mouse game, all right.

Through one of my police sources, I heard that Jim's prized and expensive chain saws were stolen from a woodlot where he and Alan had been working. More than likely, they were taken by someone Jim owed a little money to and were being held as collateral—it wasn't only the courts who never got their money from Jim.

Armed with this tidbit of information, I devised a hastily put-together plan. I went back to Jim's house to make a nuisance appearance. As before, his wife said he wasn't there, and she didn't know when he would be back. I knew damn well he probably was perched in the next room, smiling like a purring cat.

After leaving his house, I beat feet to the Pittsfield Police Department, where the stolen chain saw report had been taken. I had a plan that just might lure the big boy out of his house and into the backseat of my cruiser.

I removed my own dilapidated chain saw from my trunk and dragged it into the police station. The patrolman on duty joked, "You going to cut the trees down around here, John?"

"Nope, I'm going to execute an arrest warrant and hopefully you'll help me do it," I said, and then explained Big

Jim's little game of hide-and-go-seek in order to avoid the warrant.

I asked the patrolman to call Jim's house. Obligingly, the young officer did and was told by Jim's wife, "He isn't here, and I don't know when he'll be back."

Following the script we'd planned, the young officer said he had just recovered a chain saw from a residence in Pittsfield. "It could possibly be the one he reported stolen a while back," the officer emphasized. "Jim needs to come to our office to identify it as soon as possible, or else we are going to have to return it to the person we seized it from."

Her attitude changed. "I know where I can reach him. Just as soon as I do, we'll be right up," she said.

The officer and I exchanged big, devious grins, and the wait was on. I grabbed the arrest warrant and ducked into a small office out of sight.

Exactly as expected, Big Jim's old pickup truck, listing heavily to one side from the excessive weight of my hefty friend, came skidding into the parking lot. Big Jim maneuvered himself out of the truck with his wife following along like a puppy.

The young officer greeted them in the station lobby, holding my old blue chain saw in his hands.

"That ain't my gawd-damned chain saw," Jim grumbled. "Mine's a good one and not a mongrel like that frigging old piece of junk.

"Besides, mine is a Husqvarna—" he continued raving.

I stepped into the room.

Jim looked over at me and smiled. "I think I've been had," he said.

With a bigger grin on my face, I said, "That you have, Jim, that you have!"

I told him he was under arrest and that we were going to take a ride to Belfast together.

It was a struggle shoving the 500-plus-pound monster into the backseat of my cruiser, but somehow we managed. The car was riding mighty low as we struck out on the long ride to the Waldo County slammer.

It wasn't the last time our paths would cross. As a matter of fact, in later years there would be an incident that would take another entire book to describe.

I shouldn't admit it, but I enjoyed my run-ins with Grover and Jim and their ilk. After all, they were a big boost to my job security.

Care to Join Us in a Deer Drive?

Hunting season always provides many surprises, and more so, plenty of excitement. I often found myself hurrying from one place to another in an effort to answer complaints while at the same time trying to keep the majority of hunters in line.

One of the most common complaints we received, and one of the more difficult violations to chase down and get a conviction for, is "gang hunting," also known as a deer drive. In gang hunting, several people—the drivers—join together to force deer out of a patch of woods into the rifle sights of other members—the standers. The drivers line up in the woods a short distance apart and slowly walk toward the standers. At one time, this type of hunting was legal. But after a record number of accidental shootings during a deer drive, several of which resulted in fatalities, the Legislature outlawed the once-famous practice, much to the chagrin of many old-time hunters.

For wardens, the burden of proof to successfully obtain a conviction for a deer drive is extremely difficult. First of all, it requires a little ingenuity on the warden's part to establish that all of the hunters were hunting together as a group. The warden has to prove that members of the group had been strategically placed in designated areas, and he has to prove that those walking a few feet apart toward their friends were making an effort to herd the critters in their friends' direction.

One particular family within my district from the Jackson, Brooks, Waldo, and Knox area defiantly chose to ignore this law. Year after year they continued hunting in that same old family tradition while keeping a wary eye out for that damned old game warden—me—in the process.

I'd previously summonsed most of the family members for the violation. Some openly admitted to their guilt by entering a guilty plea through the mail to avoid a court appearance. Others, although they knew they were wrong, opted for a trial before a judge to see if I could prove my case.

In some of those trials, I was successful in my efforts, but in most of them, I was not, and a cat-and-mouse game developed between us, one that I actually enjoyed playing. I had the impression that they did, too. It was as challenging for them to outsmart the game warden as it was for them to bag a trophy buck. I admit that catching these fellows, who I enjoyed being with outside of the hunting season, became a pet project.

I heard that the group would be conducting yet another deer drive south of Brooks village on the first Saturday of the hunting season. Roughly knowing the area they'd be hunting in on that first day, I devised a plan of attack.

Early Saturday morning, my working partner, Norman Gilbert, and his son, Danny, dressed as hunters ourselves in the required blaze orange. Toting rifles, we began cruising the area with Danny driving the family's Jeep, searching for the notorious gang of deer drivers.

We soon located the boys. There were eight of them in the party; two stayed behind, while the other six entered the woods. One hunter stood on a camp road, while the other overlooked a power line. Both areas were perfect places to see anything being driven out of the woods.

Once the drivers were out of sight, I jumped out of the Jeep with my rifle in hand. I meandered into the woods, planning to walk alongside them, but at a distance, pretending to be one of the gang. I knew all of these men, and they all knew me, but I doubted they'd recognize their local warden in bright orange hunting gear, especially with a hat pulled down over his head. It was a chance I'd take.

Norman had walked down near the stander perched by the power line, acting as if he was hunting for deer along the way. The hunter said, " Hey, there, bud. Why don't you join us if you want to? We've got a deer drive coming through here. You can stand up on the other side of the road. It would be a great spot if they jump anything."

"Thanks, I will. How many of you are there?" Norman asked.

"My cousin's down on the camp road below us, and I'm watching this power line. There are six more in our group coming through the woods shortly," he replied with a grin. "If a deer should run across the road, you'd have a good chance over there!"

Norman knew the stander was trying to station him where he'd be well out of their way and would see little, if any, action. This poor fellow didn't have a clue of the surprise he had coming.

Meanwhile, there is nothing like a good admission from one of the party to strengthen the case in court. Even more so, there's nothing like having a plan actually coming together for a change.

As I walked through the brush, I kept nodding and waving to the hunter I was aligned with, receiving friendly waves back. Eventually we drivers came out on the roadway, one by one, near the power line.

No deer was driven from these woods that day. I held back a ways, as the drivers congregated along the roadway to discuss among themselves where to go next.

I heard one of them: "We want to be careful—that gawd-damned John Ford could come along at about any time now and give us his usual ration of #$@%*&."

That comment initiated a few more snippets from the group, none of them worthy of putting in print.

It was show-and-tell time. I moved into the group and piped up, "Good morning, gentlemen! I believe you're a little too late; John is already here." It was a mini-Superman moment of sorts as I peeled off my hat and jacket, proudly displaying my warden's uniform. Norman was stripping down to his uniform at the same time.

Needless to say, there were eight very somber faces, and eight court tickets later, we jumped back into the Jeep, headed for another deer drive in the making.

Norman and I had sent a message to this defiant crew that deer drives were illegal, and that they could be infiltrated by the woods cops as easily as not. Before my career ended, though, I ran across the same old gang again, doing as they had always done. Old habits are obviously hard to break, and I'm not sure in this case they ever were broken. The cat-and-mouse game was fun to play. It was more rewarding, however, when for once the mouse caught the cat for a change.

A Real Hat Trick

Sunday hunting in Maine is illegal because most residents believe they should have one day a week during November to roam freely in the woods without fear of being mistaken for a big buck.

One freezing and foggy Sunday afternoon during hunting season, I received a call from a gentleman I knew as Maynard.

Maynard lived in Troy in an area surrounded by farmland, old fields, and woods. It was in prime deer country and I knew it well. I'd met Maynard in the past, and I couldn't say we'd had the friendliest of relations. I sensed that he wasn't the biggest supporter of the Fish and Game Department, or the wardens who enforced the laws, including me.

So I was taken aback when I received the call from Maynard, asking, "How would you like to apprehend a Sunday hunter?"

Excited at the prospect of catching a violator and perhaps even gaining a little confidence in Maynard, I listened carefully to his complaint.

"Out in the far corner of my back field I just saw a hunter perched way up in a tree, waiting for a deer to come out," he said.

Chuckling, he added, "The gawd-damned fool isn't bright enough to discard his blaze-orange hunting cap. If anyone ever deserved to get caught, he does."

It was getting to be late in the afternoon. I had to hurry if I was going to make an official visit with this hoodlum up in a tree.

I hid my cruiser quite some distance away and hiked up an old woods road leading to the field. I could see the orange hunting cap in the distance, exactly where Maynard had said it would be.

I reached for my trusty binoculars, but I'd forgotten them. Damn it! All I could see was the bright orange hat bobbing up and down in the tree.

I had to get closer, so I crept along using the dense brush to conceal my presence. Occasionally, I stepped out to the edge of the field to make sure my prey was still in the tree.

At least I had sense enough to bring my flashlight, for by now it was beginning to get quite dusky. The icy mist had turned into a freezing rain, and I was shivering as I moved closer to the tree.

I wondered if this person would surrender easily, or if I'd end up in a foot chase or, even worse, with a fight on my hands. Sometimes these poachers were hell-bent on getting away from the law.

With darkness now settling over the area, what had started out as a crime of Sunday hunting had now elevated to the more serious offense of night-hunting.

I couldn't help thinking that maybe old Maynard wasn't as bad as I had figured him out to be. Maybe I'd misjudged the old boy right from the start.

I finally had worked my way as close to the tree and the hunter as I was going to get without tipping my hand. I peeked out at the tree one last time. The hat was still high in the branches. I swear I could see the fellow's body and most of his face, but I couldn't make out who it was in the darkness.

It was time to surprise this Sabbath Day criminal. I wanted to catch him way up in the air and not on the ground where he could run off.

Taking a couple of deep breaths, I shot out of the woods with my flashlight aimed directly at the spot where this nimrod was perched. I fully expected all hell to break loose, but instead the orange cap was still as I ran toward it, screaming at the top of my lungs for him to come to hell down out of that tree.

Much to my surprise, there was no hunter.

Instead, I found a blaze-orange hunting cap strategically nailed to a small tree limb.

I'd been had, big time!

I stomped around underneath that tree for the next few minutes, cursing Maynard like I'd never cursed anybody before. He had purposely lured me out of the comfort of my home and into this little booby trap.

I set out to call him up and say, "Hey, Maynard, thanks for all your help this afternoon. I never did make it up to the tree you talked about, but instead I apprehended two of your neighbors along the way. I just wanted to warn you they aren't too happy with you," and then simply hang up. But I thought better of it.

I could just picture the old coot, curled up on his couch watching a football game and snickering to himself, thinking of my cold and frosty arse out in the woods nearby.

Now that was a real "hat trick."

Good News, Bad News!

An informant told me that Roy was peppering the countryside with a string of unlabeled traps as he cruised the backcountry on a small trail bike.

I decided to start my search near his house, which was surrounded by several large fields and a variety of woods roads that would take him out into the backcountry. Sure enough, I found bike tracks skirting the edge of the fields. It was a foggy October day as I began following the tracks through the fields.

The tracks appeared to be fairly fresh, but it was hard to tell just how fresh. Then, a short distance in front of me, I saw the bike parked at the edge of the woods. I ducked off to one side, waiting for Roy to return.

It wasn't long before he came out of the woods, climbed aboard the little trail bike, and headed my way. I stepped out in front of him, motioning for him to stop.

He was surprised to see me, to say the least. "Hi, John," he said. "What the hell are you doing way out here?"

"I was about to ask you the same thing," I said, noting a small basket filled with trapping equipment attached to the bike.

Roy was toting a holstered weapon on his side. I asked if it was loaded. "It is," he sheepishly replied.

"Do you have a concealed weapon permit that allows you to carry a loaded weapon?" I inquired.

"No, I don't," he sputtered.

"Well, Roy, you legally can't carry a loaded weapon on a motor vehicle," I informed him. "And what about these traps you're setting; are they all legal, properly tagged with your name and address?"

"I think so. I might have forgotten some, but I don't think I did."

"Well, Roy, the reason I ask is that recently I've seized several unlabeled traps scattered around the area. My information is that they belong to you and your brother. I'd strongly suggest you guys might want to make sure you're abiding by the rules. How about the one you've just placed down here—is it all legal?" I inquired.

"I'm not sure," he said. Just from his actions, I knew it wasn't.

I passed Roy a couple of summonses along with the suggestion that he might want to consider retracing his trapping route, paying more attention to the rules, before I got there first. I made it clear that I'd be watching him from afar, seizing any traps I found that weren't legal.

We parted company on a fairly friendly note, all things considered. Roy assured me that he understood my warning and made a halfhearted promise that he would rectify the problem. I took him at his word.

A week later, I received another secret message from a local trapper. "Do you want to capture Roy for trapping illegally?" he asked.

I explained that I had just done so the week before. Did he have something new to offer?

"I sure do. And it's a good piece of information. I know where you can find one of his traps. It doesn't have a tag on it, but I know how you can prove that it's his!" the caller chirped.

"How do you propose that I'm going to be able prove it?"

"Well, John, lying alongside the illegal trap is his wallet. His identification and a good amount of money are inside. I didn't remove it, but I'll be glad to show you exactly where it is, and you can take it from there. Ain't no way he'll be able to deny the trap is his," he said.

"Damn it all," he went on, spluttering. "These guys just don't care about the rules. They start way too early and they trap long after the season is over. I for one am gawd-damned sick and tired of it. I know you're trying to do your best, but you need help. I'm willing to give you that help."

I met with the informant later that day, and together we hiked up Pond Hill in Brooks to an area where the familiar bike tracks were evident. He led me out through the woods to the sprung trap. Sure enough, on the ground beside it was the wallet, holding a decent amount of cash.

Thank God this man was as honest as the day is long. Others would have kept the cash and tossed the wallet.

The next day I showed up at Roy's house. He met me in the dooryard.

"What now? Damn it, I took your advice and cleaned up my act," he assured me.

Calmly I said, "Roy, I have some good news for you and I have some bad. Which would you prefer first?"

"Well, I can't imagine anything being too bad, so what's the good news?" he asked.

"Have you lost your wallet recently?"

A look of relief appeared on his face. "I did lose it, a day or two ago. All of my licenses and stuff are in it. Do you have it, I hope?"

"I do, I have it right here. Do you know how much money you were carrying when you lost it?" I inquired.

"Oh, I think maybe $70 or $80," he replied.

"Well, apparently someone is being real good to you; there's $120 in it," I said, and handed him the wallet.

"Goddamn! Boy, am I glad to have that back," he gushed. "Now, what's this supposedly bad news you have?"

"Well, Roy, I found your wallet lying on the ground beside another one of your unlabeled traps up on Pond Hill in Brooks, so I've got a summons for the offense. I told you I'd be watching! I'm serious about this illegal activity, Roy, and I hope you'll take me seriously," I barked.

"I hear ya, John. I hear ya!" he said, taking the summons.

"Can I take care of this through the mail like I did the last one?" he inquired.

"I don't think they'll let you for a second offense, Roy, especially so soon after the first. I'm sure the judge is going to want to speak to you directly. Maybe he can get the point across to you much better than I'm doing," I said.

"I assure you, John, I've got the message. I'll start pulling up all of my gawddamned traps tomorrow morning."

The good news was that this time, he was true to his word.

The Improvised Lie-Detector Test

Stuck at home with the flu, I lay on the couch grumbling to myself and idly looking out the window. I saw a young man walking down Route 7 carrying a burlap bag. He stopped and looked around, as if to see if anyone was watching him, and then he jumped across the ditch and trotted behind the stone wall in front of my house.

His strange actions certainly piqued my interest, so I continued to watch as he removed a rifle from behind the wall and quickly stuffed it into the bag.

There was no doubt he was up to something illegal as he hunkered down in the bushes, hiding from the traffic going by. I slid off my couch and watched him more closely from behind my living-room curtains.

Once the traffic cleared, he scurried back to the roadway, heading toward town carrying the concealed weapon underneath his arm. By then my curiosity had gotten the best of me. Flu or not, I decided, this matter needed a little investigation.

Grabbing my shirt and coat, I jumped into my cruiser and caught up with the young man as he casually hiked along the highway. When I pulled up behind him, he glanced my way but kept walking with the bag tucked firmly beneath his arm.

Stepping out of the cruiser I yelled, "Hey, hold up for a minute, will you? I want to talk to you."

He slowly made his way back to my car. "What do you want to see me for?" he asked nervously.

"Well, for starters, I'm a bit curious as to what you're carrying in that burlap bag there."

"Oh, it's nothing much. Just a little gift I got from a friend of mine last night," he said.

"Really," I said. "What kind of a gift is it?"

By now I'd taken the bag from him and put it on the hood of my car. I removed the rifle from the burlap sack.

"Hmm, a rifle," I said. "What's your friend's name, and just when did he give this to you? It looks like a real nice one."

I was trying to be friendly with the young fellow, whose name was Dale.

"I can't remember," he said, obviously growing more nervous by the minute.

"Really," I said again. "Well, Dale, have you had this rifle with you since last night?"

"Yup, he gave it to me last night, and now I'm heading home with it. I've had it with me all the time."

If I hadn't known he was lying it would have been obvious as he fidgeted and began to sweat.

I asked Dale to have a seat in my cruiser and I put the unloaded rifle on the backseat.

I said, "Dale, I just watched you retrieve this rifle from behind the stone wall a short distance up the road. So let's be honest—you haven't had it with you all the time, have you?"

"It wasn't me you saw, no-siree! I've had this with me ever since last night," he muttered.

I decided I'd better read him his Miranda rights in case he made some incriminating statements. After all, criminals have to be afforded every opportunity in the world to protect themselves from us damned old cops, and the Miranda procedure was a requirement of that process.

Having understood his rights, Dale said he was more than willing to speak to me or any other officer without having an attorney present. "I've got nothing to hide," he said.

His hands trembled. He couldn't look me in the eye. That alone is usually a good indication that a person is being less than truthful.

I called the State Police barracks to ask that a trooper start my way. I planned to turn the matter over to them. Feeling as miserable with the flu as I did, the last thing I cared to deal with was some bonehead who might be involved in criminal activity.

Within moments, the Chevy Chase of the Maine State Police, Trooper Greg Myers, came skidding up with his emergency lights flashing.

Those of us who worked with Greg never knew what to expect when we were around him. His reputation of being a rebel cowboy in a police uniform was well documented. Department protocol and professionalism weren't his greatest attributes by any means, but he was extremely good at his job and a whole hell of a lot of fun.

Greg was a stocky character, willing to tackle an entire gang of sumo wrestlers by himself if warranted. I knew the minute he arrived that I was in for a treat. As usual, he didn't let me down.

His uniform hat straddled the back of his head, and he gripped his holster like Wyatt Earp preparing for a battle at the O.K. Corral as he stepped out of his cruiser and came our way.

He stared at my passenger with a look that would've scared the hell out of any normal person. I looked at Dale and beads of sweat were actually rolling down his face. "What the hell is he doing here?" Dale asked.

"Well, Dale, I think your story is just a little unbelievable, and I'm turning you over to Waldo County's top cop," I explained.

I later learned that Greg was quite familiar with Dale and his lengthy history of criminal activity. Within minutes after explaining to Greg what I'd seen, he pulled one of the corniest investigative tactics I'd ever seen.

Knowing that Dale had waived his rights, Greg said, "Dale, I think you're lying to us. Would you be willing to take a polygraph test?"

"Damn right I would," Dale said. "I ain't hiding nothing!"

"Good," Greg replied. "I happen to have a portable polygraph machine right here in my cruiser, and I can give you the test right now."

I joined them in Greg's cruiser, about to witness one of the greatest shows on earth. Dale was wiggling around in the front seat like a slimy night crawler trying to make an escape.

Greg reached in back and removed a case that contained a portable radar unit used to catch speeders. I caught a devilish smirk on his face and a devious little wink of the eye, indicating he was about to pull another classical Greg moment. To think I was going to witness it brought a huge smile to my face. Suddenly, I wasn't feeling quite so flu-ish.

Greg put the radar unit together and plugged it into the car's electrical system. Then he held the cone of the radar in front of Dale and calmly explained, "Dale, this is a portable lie-detector unit. You can't fool it no matter how hard you try. If you're telling us the truth, you can take your rifle and walk away from here a free man. If not, I'll be able to tell, and remember, Dale, the machine never lies. You have to speak right directly into this cone, and if it makes a beeping noise that means you are lying. If it makes no noise, you are being truthful. Do you understand?"

"Yes, sir," Dale muttered.

"Okay, Dale, here we go. Let's start with your full name," Greg asked, placing the cone beneath Dale's chin. Dale leaned forward, staring directly at the instrument being shoved in his face. He loudly stated his name. The machine never made a peep.

"Good so far," Greg said.

Greg asked a few more questions unrelated to the reasons we were there. Again there was complete silence from the unit.

Dale seemed to be enjoying his moment of truthfulness. He grew more and more relaxed. I'm sure he was thinking that soon he'd be walking away from this latest intrusion upon his freedom.

Then came the moment I was anticipating. Greg sternly inquired, "Dale, who gave you that rifle?"

"I don't remember his name."

The machine began squealing and beeping like crazy. It was, of course, Greg fooling with the squelch.

"Want to try again, Ace?" Greg demanded. "You flunked that one badly. Did you steal this rifle?"

"No, sir, I didn't. I found it," he stuttered. His voice was trembling. His hands were shaking like a bowl of Jell-O. Again, the machine bleeped and squealed. It was a deafening noise. The loud burst even caused me to jump.

Within a few minutes, Dale had experienced enough of Greg's lie-detector test.

"Okay, okay, you got me," he shouted. "I stole the rifle last night at a party up the road. I hid it in a stone wall near there and I came back today to pick it up. I don't know why I did it. It was the stupidest damn thing I ever did."

He whimpered as he finally confessed.

In the end, as wacky as it might have been, justice was served. We traced the rifle's rightful owner, who happened to be my neighbor. I contacted him while he was vacationing in Florida to tell him we'd recovered his stolen rifle.

"What stolen rifle?" he asked.

Much to his surprise, I told him what had transpired at his home while he was away.

It's not often that a crime gets resolved before it's even reported. This happened to be one of those rare moments. Thanks to being in the right place at the right time, and, of course, a little creative ingenuity from a rebel Maine state trooper, justice had once again prevailed.

Cat Got Your Tongue?

Chet and Katherine were an elderly couple who lived in a decaying farmhouse in South Unity. They were part of an informal network of contacts I had developed in my patrol area, and I visited them on occasion to catch up on the local scuttlebutt.

In his heyday, Chester was an avid hunter, and he had plenty of stories to tell. I had come to the conclusion that he didn't obey most of the rules governing the sport, but then again, hunting was in many cases a matter of family survival. People had to fend for themselves back then. They would not accept handouts: It was a matter of personal pride and integrity for these folks to survive on their own, and they wanted it left that way.

Farmers like Chet assumed they had a right to occasionally poach a deer as long as they didn't get caught, and they knew their neighbors would never tell. The meat was never wasted or sold, nor did they run around the community bragging about their harvests. After all, why shouldn't they take a critter every now and then? It was the poor farmer who usually ended up feeding the deer and other wild creatures from the land they maintained and the crops they raised. With all the grief these folks endured, they should be entitled to an occasional deer, even if it was illegal.

That's what Chet told me, anyway, over and over, sometimes directly, sometimes through his stories. I didn't argue with him, just listened.

Even more than Chet loved to talk about the past, Kate loved her cats. There were easily a dozen or more of the furry critters scurrying about, some perched on a windowsill, others lolling on the kitchen table. The couch was covered with a large sheet of cardboard to protect it from the many cats sprawled on top of it. Scattered throughout the home were layers of cat hair and feces, along with the putrid smell associated with so many of these furry felines.

I dreaded stopping for any length of time during my visits, but I knew these old folks enjoyed an occasional call from their local woods cop, and I liked talking to them, too.

During one visit, as Chet was telling stories of days gone by, Kate piped up, "Chet and I were just about ready to have a cup of coffee, John. Won't you join us?"

"What the hell, I'm not going anywhere;, I'd love a cup," I answered.

Chester was sputtering about the many struggles of performing the endless chores on the farm. All the while, those damned old cats seemed to be sizing me up. Some of them kept jumping into my lap while others simply purred off in the distance, watching my every move.

I didn't dare tell Chet and Kate how much I despised cats. I viewed all feline beasts as independent creatures with highly developed killer instincts. In reality, they are responsible for killing more small-game animals than all the trappers in the area combined.

Kate's cats obviously sensed my dislike for them, so they kept bothering me. Noting my obvious attempts to brush them away, Chet shouted, "Knock them to hell upside the head if they get to bothering you too bad. The gawd-damn critters!"

It was apparent that he didn't share Kate's compassion for cats either.

"Coffee's ready!" she hollered.

Kate served the coffee in heavy pottery mugs, capable of holding a much larger quantity of coffee than your regular cup.

"What do you want in your coffee, John?" she inquired.

"Oh, just a little cream, Kate, that'd be good." I smiled politely.

I hoisted the big mug to my lips and took a big sip of the piping-hot brew.

All of a sudden, I felt a large lump of something solid against the roof of my mouth. It obviously wasn't coffee.

Something foul had been floating in my cup and now it was in my mouth. What was I going to do? I couldn't just spit it out; the last thing I wanted to do was embarrass my elderly friends.

But what could the lumpy object in my mouth be? I swirled it from one side of my mouth to the other, trying to figure it out. Could it be a cat's hairball, or even worse, a gob of cat dung? Oh, God, just the thought was making my stomach turn. I have to tell you, I am not the strongest person in the world when it comes to something gross like this.

All the while, I was trying not to let the old couple know of the crisis I found myself in, or the horrible thoughts that were on my mind.

Reluctantly, I closed my eyes and swallowed the mouthful of coffee and its horrid contents. Down the hatch it went, thankfully not scraping and fetching up in my throat along the way.

I swear, during this entire fiasco I glanced over at one of those damn cats and it appeared to have a big grin on its face.

I hesitantly drank the rest of the coffee, planning to make a hasty departure as soon as I could. I thought I was going to be sick.

I left the farm soon afterwards, relieved to be out in the fresh air once again. As I drove away, I began gagging and heaving, thinking about what possibly could be settling in my stomach. The next thing I knew, I was standing outside the cruiser, vomiting in the ditch along the side of the road.

Now I know this is gross, but I took a stick and began intently examining the contents dumped upon the ground, hoping to find the cause of my discomfort.

I didn't find anything, and to this day, I don't have a clue what it was that slid down my throat.

I still believe those damned old cats—staring, grinning, and sizing me up—had something to do with my tainted coffee. I just know it!

Needless to say, my dislike for cats became even more intense from that day forward. It also made me think twice about when and where I would accept a cup of coffee— especially if there were any cats nearby.

Here, kitty, kitty! Here kitty, kitty, I've got a little something for you!

Are You Lonesome Tonight?

How many of you can recall exactly where you were and what you were doing when you found out Elvis had left the building for the last time? I can tell you exactly where I was on August 16, 1977, when he died—who I was with, and what we were doing.

I didn't hear about the King's passing until late that evening. Sergeant Bill Allen and I were hunkered down in a remote field in Brooks, waiting for a poacher to venture our way.

We were listening to the radio, to the many accolades and tributes pouring in from all over the world as word quickly spread of the King's untimely death at an age when he should have been in his prime.

I remember trying to come up with the words to "Are You Lonesome Tonight?" I even thought I could create my own version of the song. Something like:

Are you lonesome tonight?
With your gun and blue light?
Are you sorry we're out here, alone . . . "

But I figured Bill would all but kill me if I started to sing it, so I smartly chose to remain silent.

Then I thought of my dear departed grandmother.

I hate to admit my age, but I was a teenybopper when Elvis Aaron Presley climbed the throne as the King of Rock 'n' Roll and became one of the greatest entertainers ever. I vividly recall the hysteria as the long-haired, hip-swiveling, crowd-wooing entertainer made his debut. Adults boisterously exhibited a constant barrage of disgust over the actions and songs coming from the young man—a handsome lad who drove the girls crazy and caused many young men to impersonate his every move.

Some folks were quick to compare Elvis's antics to those of a deadly epidemic sweeping uncontrollably throughout the country and beyond. My beloved grandmother was one of them, may her soul rest in peace. She constantly attempted to instill into my pea-brain the idea that this performer's actions were evil and that I should not allow myself to submit to such treasonous and evil shenanigans.

She never realized that I happened to hear her peacefully rocking on her porch one day humming "Are You Lonesome Tonight?" Another time, I caught her tapping her toes as she hummed "(I Just Wanna be Your) Teddy Bear."

Of course, being the devious devil I was, I couldn't resist making my little secret a point of high interest at Christmastime. I searched for the cutest, cuddliest, most irresistible teddy bear I could find. I attached a card to its chest that read, "I Just Wanna Be Your Teddy Bear," then neatly wrapped it in a beautiful Christmas package. I couldn't wait until the entire family was gathered around the Christmas tree, including aunts, uncles, cousins, and the like, watching as Gram opened my gift. I clued in everybody in advance, making them well aware that although Gram constantly griped about Elvis and his swiveling hips, I had, on more than one occasion, found her out to be a fan.

The moment of truth arrived when she tore into the wrapping paper. I can still see her face when that little teddy bear with the attached note fell into her lap. Without any hesitation, she clutched it to her breast and began humming the now-famous "Teddy Bear."

From then on, Gram said nothing more about the swiveling hips, the chaos, or the evilness that she believed the King portrayed. For years, she had that little teddy bear perched in her bedroom. It was her favorite gift and remained as such until the day when she left this great world of ours.

Back on the stakeout, Bill and I suddenly saw headlights coming up the field road and into the spot where we were working. No one had any reason to be there, unless, of course, they were night-hunting. A large pickup truck drove around the huge field, flashing a bright handheld spotlight from one end of the field to the other. They obviously had one thing in mind, and it wasn't looking for Elvis.

In typical night-hunting fashion, they searched every crook and cranny of the field, hoping to see the shining eyes of a deer in their bright beam of light. Little did they know we were glued to their back bumper like a bumper sticker, following them everywhere they went, waiting for the right moment to make our presence known. We watched as three adult heads intently followed the beam of light around the field.

It was show-and-tell time. Bill snapped on the headlights, the siren, and the blue lights, signaling for them to stop. But instead of heeding the command, they led us on a brief chase out through the tall grass, spinning and sliding around like the Dukes of Hazzard being pursued by the fat little sheriff, all the while frantically tossing evidence out the window.

"There goes the light!" Bill yelled.

"Ooo, ooo, ooo, there goes the gun," we both shouted, as a rifle sailed out into the grass.

They skidded to an abrupt halt with us nearly cleaning off the back end of their pickup.

Amazingly, we found two men, a woman holding her yearling child firmly in her lap, and the family dog, all crammed into the passenger compartment of the truck. This was a real family affair, for sure.

So there you have it, ladies and gentlemen—after the tragic end of the King's life here on Earth, life went on for others. While Elvis tributes crammed the airwaves, evil still reigned. But justice ultimately prevailed, and Bill and I were not in the least lonesome on that particular night.

Smoke Gets in Their Eyes

Late one winter evening I received a tip concerning the upcoming activities of a couple of young men from Unity, Gary and Mike, who I'd had occasion to know fairly well. It seems this pair was planning a late-night trip out to Mixer Pond in the town of Knox with the intention of illegally fishing for a mess of freshwater smelts.

Neither man had the required bait dealer's license that would have authorized them to legally fish for smelts. Without this license, all fishing on this frozen body of water after dark was illegal.

It was obvious these two numbskulls knew they were breaking the law. They went so far as to put tar paper over the windows of their ice shack so they wouldn't draw the attention of anyone on shore. They had little to worry about, seeing that there was only one family inhabiting the entire area.

Their actions certainly fell short of being the crime of the century. As a matter of fact, I didn't plan on taking any legal action unless, of course, they were decimating the stock of smelts in the pond, which I seriously doubted.

But I wanted to teach these characters a lesson, letting them see firsthand how their local warden didn't work a normal schedule like most folks.

This cold winter night was exceptionally bright with a near-full moon that made sneaking across the pond an easy chore. I watched from the shoreline until I was sure the two fishermen were perched comfortably inside their ice shack. Then, quietly, I shuffled across the black ice in the bright moonlight, coming in on the back side of their little shanty.

They didn't hear me as I crept up to the hut. I could hear them chatting and joking inside the camp as they got their woodstove going, popped open some cans—beers, I assumed—and then tried to jig a smelt or two.

I'm sure they felt they were completely alone in God's little paradise, underneath the bright moon and out of the frosty air. No other bait dealers were on the pond, probably because it was so cold and the moon was so bright it might have an effect on the smelts. It was a little mind-boggling knowing a damned old game warden would be out on such a night, but then again, this warden was on a mission.

The smoke poured out of the ice shack chimney as I listened to their constant chatter inside. They apparently were having no luck, joking inside the camp, "Here fishy, fishy! Where are you, fishy?" But they sure seemed to be enjoying themselves, as the tops of the beer cans continued popping and the empties kept hitting the wooden floor.

They definitely weren't catching any fish, so I decided to have a little fun. Leaned up against the back of the ice shack was a small pine board. I gently slid it over the top of the chimney to prevent the smoke from escaping. Within seconds the men began coughing and gagging inside as the shanty quickly filled with smoke.

Gary started yelling, "What the hell is wrong with this damned woodstove? I'll go outside to see if the chimney is plugged. Tell me if it clears up."

Hurrying, I removed the board off the top of the chimney and I stepped around the opposite side of the shack. I heard Gary muckling onto the stovepipe, cranking it to a new position, all the while sputtering and grumbling about this miserable inconvenience.

From inside Mike yelled, "It's getting better, Gary—I think you got it!" Gary sauntered back into the shack, still coughing and hacking from the smoke he'd inhaled.

A few minutes later they were laughing and joking like before and begging the smelts to start biting. They'd left the door of the shack open to clear the smoke out, and now they were griping about how cold it was. Gary shoved another stick or two of firewood into the stove.

I waited a few minutes before placing the board back over the top of the stovepipe. Much coughing and gagging recurred, and Gary ran out again.

"What the #$@%*& is wrong with this #$@%*& stove? There isn't a bit of wind to interfere with that #$@%*& chimney, and the pipe seems to be clear," he said.

I pulled the board away, ducking back around the corner.

"You've got it, Gary, it's clearing up again! I think it's okay," Mike hollered.

"I don't know how to hell it could be, I didn't do anything to it yet!"

He went back inside. More beer cans popped.

I waited a few more minutes before I decided to bring this event to a head, sliding the board up over the top of the chimney one last time.

I don't dare print the roaring rendition of cusswords that flowed from inside the camp as they both came screaming toward the back of the shack, heading straight for the chimney.

This time, when they rounded the corner, I was standing there, my arms folded and a big grin on my face.

"Evening, gentlemen. Are we doing a little illegal night-fishing?"

Their screams echoed throughout the area like a wild animal being torn apart by a vicious predator. It was enough to start a pack of coyotes howling in the hills far off in the distance. In a split second, the peace and tranquility of that cold, bright moonlit night out on Mixer Pond had come to a rather abrupt end.

I didn't have the heart to write tickets for the minor violation they'd committed. And, had I chosen to write a summons, how could I possibly explain to the judge that I had to smoke them out of the camp in order to make a bust?

I do think, however, that Gary and Mike learned their lesson quite well. In reality, they were just a couple of good old boys, simply trying to get a mess of smelts and have a little fun. No harm done. Lesson learned. Mission accomplished.

My pay for the night was a whole lot of personal satisfaction and sharing a beer with Gary and Mike as they closed up their camp. We all hiked off the pond together.

Excuse Me, Ma'am

Car-deer accidents are the bane of a game warden's existence. They happen frequently, and always at an inconvenient time. We have to respond, write a report for the insurance company, and dispose of the carcass if the driver doesn't want it.

One June morning at five, the dispatcher sent me to Route 137 in Knox, where a trucker had nailed a doe, leaving her two fawns orphaned. I found him desperately trying to locate the little creatures when I arrived.

Trying to catch a healthy young fawn is comparable to roping a steer at a rodeo with a ball of thread. These little critters instinctively seek cover, remaining motionless and undetectable in the woods. You'd have to all but step on them before you could spot one.

Should they be located, capturing them was an even bigger chore, like chasing a speeding bullet through thick puckerbrush, hoping it will slow down for a tackle. But in order to appease this distraught trucker, I felt the least I could do was make an attempt to find the fawns.

The road was devoid of homes or any other signs of civilization. The woods were fairly dense along the east side where the doe's carcass lay in the ditch. The other side of the roadway was more open, with raspberry bushes and small alders covering a knoll.

"They're so damned small," the trucker said of the fawns. "I don't see how they could possibly hide so quickly."

"Mother Nature provides a means of protecting them," I assured him. "I bet they've sought shelter nearby and are hunkered down for the duration. It's really like looking for a needle in a haystack."

I had an idea. "Maybe if we drag the carcass up along the edge of the woods, they'll get hungry and return, looking for their mother," I said, though I seriously doubted that would happen.

The proposal seemed to appease the trucker, however, especially after I promised to frequently patrol through the area to see if the little fawns might reappear.

I completed the required paperwork, and we went our separate ways.

During the day, I made several trips through the area, hoping to see the critters standing along the edge of the woods near the carcass. Other than the normal flow of traffic passing through, though, I saw nothing.

Late in the afternoon, I made another pass. A car was parked directly across the road from the dead doe. Both doors were wide open. I could see two women in the thick raspberry bushes and alders a short distance from their car.

Aha, I said to myself. They've spotted the fawns and they're trying to catch them.

I stopped the cruiser, got out, and ran up to where the two women were squatted down in the bushes.

They screamed and shouted a barrage of obscenities, while at the same time demanding that I get the hell away from them. Oblivious to their entreaties, I continued rushing into the brush, hoping to give them a hand in capturing the fawns.

It wasn't until I was within a few feet of the women that I realized they weren't pursuing a couple of orphaned fawns—far from it. Instead, they'd stopped along this remote section of highway in order to relieve themselves. Oh, my freaking word, what was I going to do now?

"Just who to hell do you think you are, you sick son of a bitch," one of them screeched at the top of her lungs while she desperately tried to pull her pants up. I realized I was in quite a pickle, one that would require a lot of luck and diplomacy to escape unscathed.

By now, the other lady had a death grip on a large chunk of deadwood, meaning to use it as a weapon should I stray her way.

As quickly as I'd entered their sacred territory, I found myself backtracking even quicker.

I noticed the New Hampshire plates on their car. Perhaps I should have scooted back into my cruiser just as fast as my fat little legs would carry me, hop into my warden's wagon, and take off. But I knew that wasn't the professional way to handle the situation. The women would just end up calling the State Police, and then everyone would be on a manhunt for my cruiser and me.

My face was as red as a lobster straight out of a boiling pot. I desperately tried to reassure them that I was an officer of the law, but they would have no part of it.

"We know about guys like you! You're not always who you claim to be," the ladies angrily bellowed as they continued adjusting their pants.

"Honestly, I can explain what's going on here, ma'am."

"I'm sure you can! You guys always have a slick answer for your warped actions," the one nearest said.

"Please, let me try," I said as I continued backing out toward the road.

"This better be some gawd-damned good," she yelled, demanding to know my name and badge number. "You haven't heard the end of this by any means, you sorry son of a bitch!"

"I don't blame you, ma'am, but please hear me out before you rush to judgment," I pleaded.

By now they were scurrying back toward the safety of their parked car. One of them still had a death grip on the big stick, watching my every move to make sure I wasn't going to jump her.

I tried explaining the situation from earlier that morning, even offering to show them the deer carcass across the road, if they cared to see it.

I might just as well have been talking to a couple of rocks. Neither of them heard a single word I said, and they obviously wanted to get as far away from the likes of me as possible.

Needless to say, once they reached their car, they shot out of the area like a missile. I expected at any minute I'd hear a broadcast over the State Police radio, "All units! All units! Be on the lookout for a white male, wearing a warden's uniform, and driving a green Plymouth in the vicinity of Payson Hill in Knox. This male is wanted for—"

Thank God, no distress call or complaints were made. Business for the rest of the day went on as usual.

I decided after this little experience that in the future I'd spend a little more time thinking things through before running into the bushes to see what was going on. It may be difficult to round up a pair of fawns, but that would be a picnic compared to answering to a couple of wet hens.

Just for the record, the poor little fawns never were seen again. I assume they took shelter somewhere in the thick woods, with death their likely destiny. At times, Mother Nature can be cruel—without a doubt, this was one of those times. I know I'd confronted a couple of women who could have been just as brutal had they been given the chance.

One Man's Tragedy Saves Another Man's Life—Mine

Late in the afternoon of June 1, 1988, two men capsized their canoe on small Bowler Pond in the town of Palermo. One of the men made it safely to shore, but the other was presumed to have drowned.

The next day, warden divers located the body of the young victim on the bottom of the pond. Another warden and I pulled the body up into the boat. Suddenly, I felt sharp pains in my side, but I brushed off the discomfort as merely straining a muscle or two during the lifting effort.

It was my job to deliver the body to the funeral home, fill out the official paperwork, and notify the victim's family members. The pain in my side continued, but for the time being it was tolerable.

The next day, the pain was worse. I decided to venture to the emergency room at the Belfast hospital.

"Mrs. Ford won't have to worry about cooking supper tonight, John," Dr. John Gage, a family friend, informed me with a big smile.

"Why's that?" I inquired.

"It appears you've got appendicitis. I want you in the operating room in about fifteen minutes," he replied.

The pain was getting worse by the minute, and the doc's diagnosis sounded plausible. I wasn't worried about the procedure. Hell, it was a routine operation and I'd be out working after a day or two of recuperation.

Hours later, as I slowly awoke from the anesthesia, I saw my friendly doc standing over me. This time, unlike his big, earlier smile, he was sporting a look of concern.

"What's up?" I groggily inquired.

"I don't know how to tell you this, John, but your appendix was not the issue. Once we operated, we found an inflamed lymph node pressing against your appendix. I'm concerned as to its size and mass, so I've removed it for a biopsy," he said. "It may be nothing, but it possibly could be a form of lymphatic cancer. We won't know for a few days. Let's wait until the results come back and go from there."

My mind started to race like never before. During my law enforcement career, when confronted with serious situations, I dealt with them on my own and by instinct. Now, the possibility of confronting the "big C" was totally out of my control. Instead, I'd be totally relying on the professionals and my Christian faith, hoping to beat the odds, whatever those odds might be.

What should I expect? How would I deal with the possibility of succumbing to a disease that had claimed the lives of so many before me? What about young John? Would I see my son graduate from high school? Would I see him grow into manhood, get married, raise a family of his own? What about Mrs. Ford? What would she do? Would I become a burden on her? A constant barrage of "what-ifs" were running through the mush-pit between my ears.

I just wanted to go back to sleep, hoping the next time I opened my eyes this all would've been nothing more than a bad dream.

A few days later, I received the official news: The inflamed node was malignant. It was like receiving a message from the Grim Reaper himself. Life as I knew it would never be the same.

Trying to explain to my twelve-year-old son the gravity of the situation we as a family now faced was heart-wrenching. Fear of the unknown was the most difficult issue. I

Courtesy of John Ford Sr.

John Ford Sr. with his son, John Jr.

wasn't worried so much about myself as about what my precious family would have to endure. But to say I wasn't scared, discouraged, or depressed would be nothing but a damn lie. Personally, I was petrified.

And, like so many before me who had received the same devastating news, I asked, "Why me?" Then, "How much do I want to put everybody through, knowing what the end results could be?" Admittedly, the thought of suicide ran through my mind as I wondered, rather irrationally, if I really wanted to go through with the medical treatment and put my family through a living hell over a long period of time when the end results more than likely would be the same.

Fortunately, once the initial shock was over, some form of sanity returned. By the damn, I was only forty-one years old—too young to give up the charmed life I'd been living.

The battle lines were drawn. The best cancer doctors in eastern Maine, Drs. Segal and Hartz, drew up a course of action, and I committed my full trust and support. I wasn't giving up—I'd be a fighter, and my faith in the Almighty became stronger.

I was stabbed and penetrated in ways I never would have imagined, as X-rays and a host of other tests were conducted to see how widespread my disease had become. Fortunately, all of the test results were coming back in my favor.

The entire team of medical experts agreed to one sad fact—that had I not irritated the lymph node as I had by pulling the drowning victim's body up into the boat, I might never have learned about this disease until it had spread far more than it already had. In essence they said, "One man's tragedy saved another man's life—yours."

On my forty-second birthday I started weekly barrages of chemotherapy, poisoning my body almost to the brink of death. My immune system was being completely wiped out. Every third treatment was a bummer. I found myself making mad, passionate love to the toilet bowl at least once every hour for twenty-four hours. I vomited so violently that the blood vessels burst around my eyes. Pathetically, I looked like a hybrid raccoon for a few days afterwards. My hair fell out in clumps, my taste buds had all but disappeared, my face was bloated, and I was experiencing a constant numbness in my fingers and feet.

Through it all, though, there was still time for a little humor. I was at an accident scene in Freedom assisting with traffic control, and I was wearing the dreaded warden hat that in the past I'd so desperately despised—I don't like wearing hats at all. This time, though, wearing it was a means of covering up what few clumps of hair I had remaining.

A friend happened by my location just as I lifted my hat to brush my brow. "Holy o' cripe man, who to hell gave you that horrible haircut?" he asked.

"I got it from God," I replied. "I'm going through chemotherapy, and it's the best he can do for now!"

The poor guy was so embarrassed and apologetic it was pathetic. We both chuckled about it afterwards, and we still do to this very day. It's never a bad thing to share a little humor, no matter how severe the circumstances are.

During this ordeal, then-chief Warden Larry Cummings was perhaps my greatest confidant and supporter. Sadly, Larry had the very same dreaded disease as I did. We often leaned on each other, trying to make the best out of our bad situations by offering each other rays of hope, hoping that someday this would all be behind us.

As the boss, Larry was adamant in regard to my working habits. "Do whatever you feel you can handle, John, and don't overdo it. If you get tired, just go home and call it a day," he advised. It was a big relief knowing just how supportive the agency and my brother wardens were. The warden service definitely was a great outfit to work for.

Once a week from June through September I spent hours sitting in a hospital chair with the chemotherapy slowly dripping into my veins. On October 6, 1988, the treatments came to an end. Slowly my hair started growing back. My taste buds returned, and so did my stamina.

It was like a gift from heaven when Dr. Segal told me I'd beaten the odds. For now, the disease appeared to be in remission. I needed regular monthly checkups, blood work, and an occasional CT scan, but for the time being, life as I'd known it before would somewhat return.

"If you can go five years without this type of cancer rearing its ugly head again, the odds are very good you'll never have any problems with this type of cancer down the road," I was assured by the pros.

Larry's cancer also went into remission, but it returned with a vengeance, and the end results we both had dreaded claimed yet another victim. The warden service lost its top commander, a good man, and a devoted father. I lost a true friend, along with my reassurances of being in remission. Would I be next?

Six years later my cancer did return. This time the treatments were far more intrusive and invasive, more complicated, and amazingly more effective. In the interim, I had retired from the Warden Service and assumed the duties of county sheriff, eagerly embarking upon a new career.

Once again, death was knocking at my front door, and once again I was fortunate enough to beat the odds.

These harrowing experiences brought about an appreciation for life that most of us take for granted. Suddenly, all of those things that had seemed so important before weren't quite as important as they'd seemed.

If God knocked on my door tomorrow, well, I've been blessed. I was able to watch my son, John Jr., graduate from high school and college. I watched him marry a real sweetheart, Amy, and have watched both of them proudly as they raise their own family. I have two grandchildren, Lucas and Elizabeth, who are the loves of my life. And most importantly, I have a wife, Judy, who has stood by our many trials and tribulations in a way that makes her the true hero of the family. God bless the wardens' wives, for they put up with far more than what most women are expected to. Judy was my salvation.

Finally, I was fortunate to have found a world full of friends and associates, including many over the years whose paths crossed with mine when they shouldn't have.

If there's a lesson to be learned from all of this, it's to enjoy each day as if it might be your last. One never knows, it just might be! I know I have no regrets and many blessings. For that I am truly thankful.

An Albino Fisher? Come on, Jimbo!

As I patrolled an old dirt road one fine September day—weeks before the trapping season got under way—I came upon a car parked directly in front of me, blocking the road. The driver's side door was wide open with no one around.

As I pulled in behind it, a man came out of the woods heading my way. He was carrying a 220 Conibear, a killer trap designed mostly to catch fisher. When a fisher passes through its spring-loaded jaws in pursuit of a well-placed meal on the other side—usually a dead chicken nailed to a tree—the trap snaps shut and breaks its neck.

I was curious about why Jimbo was out here in the backcountry with a trap.

"Whatcha doing," I asked, as he put the trap in his car.

"Ahhh, nothing, really. I lost this trap last fall and I just now found it," Jimbo said, somewhat nervously. "I happened to think the other day of where I might have left it, so I decided to come out here looking for it. I want to be ready for the trapping season when it opens."

He certainly was acting a little uptight, but his answer seemed reasonable. It was enough to suit me, so I numbly said, "Gee, you were lucky to find it, huh?"

"Oh, yeah, I was real lucky," he said. Was that an expression of relief on his face, realizing I'd bought his alibi?

Later that evening, I told retired warden Milton Scribner about my brief encounter with Jimbo. Scrib, as we called him, demanded to hear every detail.

As politely as he could, Scrib said with a chuckle, "You've been seriously hoodwinked by old Jimbo, John Boy. The man gotcha, and he gotcha good. I know old Jimbo quite well and so does everybody else. That man is a snake when it comes to Fish and Game."

Scrib was on a roll now. "In my book, he's about as honest as Al Capone was back in his heyday. Lost his trap last year, my arse." He laughed loudly. "He was just setting those traps out when you came along, John, and you had him dead to rights. Mark my words, John Boy, everybody in town will hear about Jimbo making a fool out of you. That's his style, you mark my words!"

I felt as though I'd just been drop-kicked in the groin. "You mean to say he lied to me, Scrib?" I stammered.

My worst fears came true a few days later when a close buddy of Jimbo's confided, "Jimbo's at work telling everybody about what a dummy this new warden in town is. He thinks he's outsmarted you and he's bragging about lying to you about a trap he was about to set when you came along."

I felt the blood curdling in my veins—not so much for the well-deserved ribbing and hassling I'd no doubt receive from local folks, but for being so damned gullible and stupid in the first place. It was a good lesson learned. The trust I eagerly placed in my fellow sportsman was no longer there.

Jimbo quickly climbed to the very top of my most-wanted list, and I knew sooner or later I'd get my chance to repay him for his act of deceit.

I spent the next few days cruising Jimbo's neighborhood, looking for more traps or any other signs of illegal activity. I found three Conibear traps, just like the one Jimbo had been carrying out of the woods. There were no names on them, as required by law, and the season had yet to start, so I sprung them one by one, seizing them on behalf of the State.

At the end of the trapping season, trappers are required to present their hides to their local warden to be tagged in preparation for selling them. Wardens turn the information into headquarters, enabling the harvesting of fisher, fox, raccoon, beaver, otter, and other wild animals to be tracked. That tracking is the basis for regulating future seasons and harvests.

Late one evening I received a call from my buddy Jimbo, inquiring if he could bring his hides over to be tagged. Pretending that I'd forgotten our first official meeting, I invited him over.

He arrived with twelve pelts. It was a banner year for the SOB, or so he said. I wondered how legal the taking of any of these fishers had actually been. I inspected the hides, snapping the metal registration tags permanently onto each pelt. The conversation was minimal.

I never mentioned our first meeting, other than to smartly inquire, "You didn't lose any more traps this year did you, Jimbo?"

"Nope," he muttered. "Why do you ask?"

"Oh, I just happened to find several illegal ones scattered around your neighborhood. I didn't know who they belonged to."

"Nope, don't know nothing about 'em," he said.

I thought, Yeah, right, Jimbo! You're absolutely right there. You don't know nothing, period.

The last hide Jimbo passed to me to tag was completely white, not the jet black of a normal fisher pelt. The hide was still attached to the metal frame used to stretch and skin critters. Jimbo said this animal was an albino male fisher.

Understandably, considering my first meeting with the troll, my instincts told me not to trust him.

"How come this one's still attached to the stretcher," I asked.

"Oh, I wanted to make sure it was stretched and dried real good before I took it off. It's a real rarity, you know. I think it might be worth a lot of money at the fur auction, being an albino and all."

Examining the pelt, I recognized why Jimbo wanted to leave it on the stretcher. It wasn't a fisher at all. Instead, it was a white house cat that he'd killed somewhere along the line, stretching and skinning it in hopes I'd place a tag on it so he could brag to his buddies about pulling the wool over my eyes once again.

Not this time, Jimbo! Not this time! My blood boiled. I flatly refused to tag the cat.

Before he left, I said, "Jimbo, I'm wise to your damned illegal antics. You might want to be looking over your shoulder in the months and years ahead. You fooled me once, Jimbo, shame on you! You try to fool me twice and shame on me."

I knew that in due time, there'd be a day of reckoning with old Jimbo. Although it took a few years for justice to finally prevail, when it did, it did big-time.

Where's the Justice?

There was a fresh dusting of snow on the ground as Deputy Warden Scott Sienkewicz and I headed toward Burnham where an elderly woman had watched her neighbor shine a light on a small field behind his trailer. Then she heard a single rifle shot.

She said the neighbor, Randy, then scurried out the back door of his trailer to an apple tree along the edge of the woods. She watched him drag what she assumed to be a dead deer into the woods, and soon after he ran back inside the trailer, leaving the animal behind.

The old woman said these kind of shenanigans had been going on for years and she'd had enough. "There won't be a damned deer left in this area if someone don't stop him," she said.

Scott and I parked in front of Randy's trailer. I tried unsuccessfully to make contact with the man, who appeared to be perched inside but refused to come to the door.

Behind the trailer, fresh footprints in the new snow headed toward the apple tree the woman had mentioned. Around the tree, we found fresh drops of blood in the snow. Drag marks headed toward the edge of the woods.

As we began following the tracks we heard the muffled bleats of an animal in distress. Walking nearer to the woods, I was shocked to find a live deer making every effort to flee. The poor creature was unable to do so because a carefully placed shot had severed its spine, rendering it crippled and unable to move. It was one of the most pathetic sights I'd experienced to that point in my career.

We watched the frightened animal desperately trying to gather enough strength to get away from us. It was obvious the tenant in the trailer had purposely wounded the animal and left it to suffer. More than likely, he planned to put it out of its misery the next morning, just before taking it to the tagging station to be registered. Signs of rigor would not yet have settled in and the tagging agent wouldn't ask any questions as to the actual time of the kill. Randy knew exactly what he was doing.

It was a cruel act of animal abuse to say the least.

We disposed of the poor creature, dragged the carcass across Randy's lawn, and put it in my cruiser. By then, I was irate about the viciousness of this so-called hunter.

We returned to the trailer and I pounded on the door again, but my exhortations were once again ignored.

I told Scott, "Damn it all, we know he's inside; I plan on waiting him out no matter how long it takes. I'll stay here for a week if I have to; sooner or later he'll come outside. If he doesn't, I just might call a wrecker to hook onto his damned old trailer and haul the whole kit and caboodle down to the county jail!"

I was determined to make sure this fellow didn't sleep that night. If I wasn't going to, neither was he. Sadly, I kept the entire neighborhood awake, too, but I heard later that most of them liked the show. We certainly made sure my trailer-bound buddy wasn't getting the rest he'd planned.

Every fifteen minutes or so, I'd lay on the horn or blow the siren, hoping to force the issue and bring him outside. But all of my efforts were to no avail.

Finally, at a little after five, we saw movement inside. Again I pounded on the trailer door, making it very clear I intended to remain there until someone responded, even if it took weeks.

Slowly, the door opened and Randy sheepishly asked, "Are you looking for me?"

I felt like saying, "No. I'm here waiting for Christmas to come, hoping to catch Santa Claus sliding down your gawd-damned chimney." But I thought better of it.

I read him his Miranda rights. He'd been down this route several times before. He simply smiled and said, "I have nothing to say."

I wrote out a couple of summonses, assigning him a court date and a chance to get the attorney he wouldn't speak to us without.

The next day, I talked with Randy's neighbor. She was happier than a pig in poop to know he'd finally been caught. "He's been getting by with this for years," she said.

Her happiness soon disappeared. Randy pleaded not guilty and demanded a court trial, and wouldn't you know, my up-until-then-cooperative witness decided she would not, under any conditions, appear in court to testify against Randy. She feared retaliation in the neighborhood if she did.

"You did your job, John. You followed his tracks right out from the house to the deer and back again. No one else was there, no one else, so why to hell do you need me?" she angrily asked.

I tried to explain that the time the shots were fired and her personal observations were all necessary to convince the judge of Randy's guilt beyond a reasonable doubt. It also was a demand by our district attorney before he'd proceed with prosecuting the case.

But she would have no part of it. "I won't go to court and I won't testify," she emphasized. "That's all there is to it!" And she didn't.

The case was dismissed. Randy played the cards in this game of bluff and he won the hand. Defining justice, it turns out, is at least as much a technical matter as a moral one. There was no justice for anyone in Randy's deer slaying, and even less in the court's refusal to prosecute him.

Wile E. Fox Finds a Home

In those days before caller ID, you never knew what picking up the phone would lead to.

"Well, sir, my cat just came back from the woods and she had a little ball of fur in her mouth. I think it's a baby coyote," a woman said on the other end of the line. "Could you please come pick it up? Its eyes aren't even open, and it's barely moving, and I just don't know what to do with it."

I thought, Mmm, another of those damned wild animal complaints, one where some poor little critter has been plucked away from its mother.

At the same time, the idea of raising a baby coyote sounded a bit exciting.

Before long, I was holding a small, dark gray creature in the palm of my hand. It was alive but barely moving as I checked it for any damage inflicted by the cat.

Seeing none, I placed it in a small box with a bottle of hot water wrapped in a soft towel. He snuggled as close to the warmth as he could get, probably assuming his momma had returned.

At home, I prepared a larger box lined with cloth and two larger hot water bottles wrapped in cotton towels. The cardboard box would become his new home.

I decided to call this newest addition to the Ford family Wile E. Coyote—Wiley for short.

Gathering up the small baby bottles I'd used in past rehabilitation efforts, I filled them with a delicate mixture of warm evaporated milk and water. I commenced to give Wiley his first feeding away from home. The little bugger was rather hungry and quickly caught on to the feeding process.

The next day I headed to Augusta, seeking a written permit from the department to raise this most controversial animal. Many sportsmen, given the chance, would eradicate every one of them.

Chief Warden Larry Cummings typed up and authorized the rehab permit. "A coyote? That'll be an interesting critter to raise, John. Be sure to let me know how he's doing," he said.

Word spread that I was raising a baby coyote. Several inquisitive sportsmen stopped by for a look at him.

Wiley grew rapidly. His brown eyes opened, affording him the chance to observe the big world around him. By now he had developed a little personality of his own, and he scooted around in the cardboard box every time one of us came near.

After a couple of weeks, I began to see a rather strange change in Wiley's appearance. His dark gray coat was beginning to get much lighter and definitely a lot redder. And something appeared to be happening to his tail; there was a little white tip forming on the end of it. It became clear that my dream of raising a coyote wasn't going to come true. Wiley was transforming from a mean old coyote to a handsome little red fox.

Oh, boy, what was I going to tell those folks who thought I had a coyote? How could the local game warden, a person who had gone so far as to obtain a department permit to raise a wild coyote, possibly explain the grave error of wildlife misidentification? After all, wasn't I supposed to be the expert on these types of wild animals?

Wiley continued to grow rapidly. In no time, he had a handsome red coat and a big bushy tail with a bright white tip on the end. He was quite playful as he freely roamed throughout the house as if he were a puppy. He curled up by my feet or sprawled out in my lap at night as I watched television.

He followed us wherever we went in the house, always trying to find someone to play with, or someone to scratch his head and back. It was hard to refuse him, especially after looking into those handsome brown eyes.

As the summer progressed and Wiley grew, it was time to put him outdoors. I hoped he'd return to the wild where he belonged.

Courtesy of John Ford Sr.

Wiley.

He quickly established himself in the thick woods behind our house, but it didn't deter him from still wanting to be around people. Whenever we were outside, he'd run out from the woods looking for a handout of grub, or he'd grab onto some article of interest that caught his eye. He stole more than one item out of the yard, hauling them down into the woods to hide.

I recall a time when he grabbed one of Little John's brand-new sneakers, running down into the woods where he buried it in the brush. We spent two days looking for the shoe before finally finding it.

God forbid I'd leave a pack of cigarettes lying around. He'd snatch them up in a heartbeat, running off into the woods with them firmly secured between his sharp little teeth. I'd never see them again. I knew he wasn't smoking or eating them. Perhaps in a subtle kind of way, he was trying to tell me something.

Most every evening around suppertime, Wiley would leave the woods and head for our house. He would stand in front of our kitchen window waiting for us to pay attention to him, obviously seeking a meal. If we ignored him, he'd lunge feetfirst against the glass to make us aware of his presence. It was this behavior that scared the bejeezus out of more than one unsuspecting visitor as we sat around our kitchen table, chatting.

One day, I met up with the chief warden. He inquired as to how the coyote was doing.

Telling a little fib of sorts, I responded, "Oh, my coyote died, Larry, but did I tell you about the little red fox I'm raising?"

He grinned and walked away. Somehow, I think he was on to me.

With the arrival of cool fall weather, Wiley's trips from the woods to our house became less frequent. He was reverting to the wilderness, straying farther and farther away from home.

One day the phone rang. "Hi, John, this is your neighbor up the road. I just had something very strange happen in my dooryard. I shot a fox that came wandering right up to us. I think it might be rabid. What should I do with it?"

I felt a lump rise in my throat as I explained as best I could that I was quite sure the animal he killed was my own little Wiley. I don't know who felt worse, him or me.

I certainly couldn't fault the man. He had no idea I'd nurtured Wiley from his earliest days. And, his concerns were genuine. The discussions concerning rabies in our area had been widely publicized and everybody was rightly leery of a wild animal coming right up to them.

On the other hand, I couldn't force myself to go retrieve the carcass to dispose of it as I normally would. Without protesting my lack of enthusiasm to assist him, my neighbor humbly apologized, stating he understood. He would take care of it on his own.

For the next several days, I desperately found myself scanning the woods behind the house, hoping to see that magnificent little critter running through the bushes one more time. But sadly, it wasn't meant to be.

At least I had some fond memories and a few pictures of my little buddy to remind me of those good old days and the little pet who had brought so much joy to our family.

Suddenly, the Cider Didn't Taste So Good

Every fall, my friend Harold hosted a contingent of his Connecticut buddies for a deer hunt around Unity Pond.

The annual event was pretty typical for a Maine sporting getaway—big nightly meals followed by a lot of storytelling and more than a fair share of drinking and card playing, along with the many other activities a group of hunters find for entertainment while far away from home, including the occasional foray into the woods in search of a trophy deer.

Although I considered Harold a good friend, I also recognized that he wasn't the most law-abiding citizen I'd ever met, especially when he teamed up with his nonresident cronies.

We'd developed a mutual understanding. He and his pals realized I had a job to do and would show no partiality in performing my duties if they should happen to get out of line. Once that was understood, we got along fine.

Earlier in the week, I'd located one of Harold's tree stands neatly tucked away in his favorite hunting spot in South Unity. All around this tree stand were piles of apples, an obvious attempt to lure a big buck. Comically, there wasn't an apple tree within forty miles of this place.

Baiting deer is highly illegal, but it would be impossible to prove that Harold had done the dirty deed without solid evidence.

I decided to use an old trick of the trade passed along by fellow wardens whenever they found bait placed near a tree stand—they urinated on it. The human scent would deter deer from coming near the forbidden fruits.

I'd enjoyed several cups of coffee during the day, so I didn't have any problem covering Harold's many piles of apples.

Then, I firmly attached one of my business cards with a small note written on it to the seat of Harold's tree stand. "Harold, I've been here once and I'll be back!" I signed it, "I'm watching you from afar! —John"

I chuckled to myself after completing this dastardly task, extremely proud of my efforts.

A few days later, I received a call from Harold inviting me to swing by his camp the next night for supper with the gang. They had a big surprise for me, he said. It seems they'd found my warden's hat out in the field near Harold's tree stand. After supper, they planned to make a theatrical presentation of returning the hat to its rightful owner. Though I knew I would be the brunt of a joke, the thought of a good home-cooked meal was enough to entice me into making an appearance. My nightly ritual of tomato soup and crackers was starting to get old. At this point in my life, since Mrs. Ford had yet to enter the scene, I had to depend on my own cooking, which was disastrous at best.

The next evening after dark I pulled into the hunting camp. I could hear the boys loudly celebrating, bottles and glasses clanging. I was cordially greeted by the gang, especially Harold, who by now had imbibed more than enough of the liquid spirits to crank him up. No question, the campers were in a partying mood tonight. But then again, they seemed to be in that same mood every night.

Harold insisted I have a drink with the gang. Not wanting to be a prude, I reluctantly took a large glass of Harold's homemade hard cider. It was the lesser of the evils, I figured, compared to the many bottles of hard liquor lined up on the bar.

I joined the party, honestly suspecting that any of those present could become future customers in my line of work, but still, they had become friends and were fun to be around.

They couldn't wait to perform the little ceremony of presenting me with my hat. They put on a skit that was an Academy Award–winning effort for sure, including a little song and dance by the more-talented members.

Harold loudly bragged about finding my hat lying on a woods road near the old fields where he usually hunts. He assumed I was watching these fields for night-hunting activity, as he jokingly said, "Damn you, John! Now I know exactly where you park down there, and I can tell when to go there and when not to."

The group launched into a fit of laughter.

I figured it would be a good time to turn the tide on him a little bit.

"Harold!" I hollered, making sure everyone in the camp could hear me.

"What?" he replied.

"Harold, you know all those apples you dumped around that tree stand of yours in South Unity?" I shouted.

He stuttered a bit before responding: "What makes you think I dumped any apples there? Especially with all of them pine trees around there, John; they could very well be pine-apples.

"Pine-apples, that's what they are," he kept muttering, over and over. He knew damned well I couldn't prove he'd been the one to put them there.

"Well, anyway, Harold, if I were you, I wouldn't waste a lot of my precious time setting in your tree stand waiting for a big buck to show up. I peed all over those apples, and there won't be a deer within a hundred miles come to feed off them," I said.

His cronies burst into a fit of laughter that shook the entire camp. Harold looked shocked. Then, ever so drily, he responded, "John, I hate to be the one to have to tell you this, but I gathered up every one of those apples a short time before hunting season started. And I want you to know, that cider you're drinking? Well, guess where the apples came from?"

Suddenly the glass of hard cider didn't taste quite so good. By now the crew in the camp was rolling on the floor in total hysteria, and rather than laughing at Harold's expense, they were laughing at mine.

And to think it all came about because I'd lost my damned old hat in a woods road somewhere. I placed my glass on the nearest table and moseyed up to the bar where a smiling fellow poured me a healthy shot of bourbon.

About the Author

John Ford Sr., a native Mainer, was sworn in as a Maine Game Warden shortly after finishing up a four-year stint in the U.S. Air Force. He spent all of his twenty-year warden career in Waldo County in central Maine. Upon his

Courtesy of John Ford Sr.
Warden John Ford, left, shows his artwork to Warden Mike Ayer of Brewer.

retirement in 1990, he was elected as county sheriff and re-elected in 1994. He wrote a local newspaper column from 2002 into 2011, and is a regular contributor to the *Northwoods Sporting Journal*. He lives with his wife, Judy, in Brooks, Maine.